What people are saying about …

Beauty Marks

"Every woman bears a scar of some sort, and often it is a source of quiet shame and disappointment. In her newest book, *Beauty Marks*, my friend Linda Barrick gently peels back the scar to reveal the God-blessed hidden beauty and source of strength in each disappointment. As a fellow sufferer, I can attest that God's purposes behind our pain are worth every tear—the Lord and His plan for you is that good! Read this remarkable book and you will long for the true loveliness God is ready to unfold in your life! Linda shows us God's desire to turn every hurt into a heroic display of His beauty and grace. I give *Beauty Marks* a double thumbs-up!"

Joni Eareckson Tada, founder and CEO of Joni
and Friends International Disability Center

"*Beauty Marks* will take you on a healing journey that will break the power of past wounds and bitterness. You can change your thinking and actually improve the way you feel physically. *Beauty Marks* will equip and motivate you to allow God to transform your pain into passion and purpose."

Dr. Tim Clinton, president of American
Association of Christian Counselors

"From the foot of the cross to the depth of her soul, Linda takes us on a personal journey of hope and healing. As her dad, I've watched her emerge from life-threatening challenges with beauty and grace. Don't miss her powerful, passionate, and insightful biblical perspective. It will bless your heart and change your life."

Dr. Ed Hindson, dean of the School of Divinity at Liberty University

"If you've ever wondered how God could use you despite your brokenness or pain, *Beauty Marks* is for you. Linda shares incredibly helpful tips for dealing with pain and suffering, while shining a light on the One who can offer true healing: Jesus. In *Beauty Marks*, Linda reminds us all that Jesus truly can turn ashes into beauty."

Dr. Laurel Shaler, author of *Reclaiming Sanity*

"Have you faced a life-altering circumstance? We all have. Linda Barrick takes readers to the only place they can find true heart-healing—at the cross of Christ. Through the words of Jesus on the cross, Linda shares hope for a hurting world. I love her message that our scars are beauty marks that make us more of who God uniquely created us to be. Linda reminds us that if we let Him, God will use our pain, heartache, and wounds to also draw others to the healing found only in Him. This is a beautiful book we all need to help process the hard, unexpected things that happen to us and to know where to turn for hope."

Tricia Goyer, *USA Today* bestselling author of 70 books, including *Walk It Out*

Beauty Marks

LINDA BARRICK

Beauty Marks

HEALING YOUR WOUNDED HEART

David C Cook
transforming lives together

BEAUTY MARKS
Published by David C Cook
4050 Lee Vance Drive
Colorado Springs, CO 80918 U.S.A.

David C Cook U.K., Kingsway Communications
Eastbourne, East Sussex BN23 6NT, England

The graphic circle C logo is a registered trademark of David C Cook.

The website addresses recommended throughout this book are offered as a
resource to you. These websites are not intended in any way to be or imply an
endorsement on the part of David C Cook, nor do we vouch for their content.

Details in some stories have been changed to protect
the identities of the persons involved.

LCCN 2017933739
ISBN 978-1-4347-1102-1
eISBN 978-1-4347-1112-0

The Team: Alice Crider, Margot Starbuck, Amy Konyndyk, Nick Lee,
Jennifer Lonas, Abby DeBenedittis, Julie Neddo, Susan Murdock
Cover Design: James Hershberger

Printed in the United States of America
First Edition 2017

2 3 4 5 6 7 8 9 10 11

110617

*To my daughter, Jennifer, who shows me every
day what it means to have childlike faith.*

*To my sister, Christy, for her wisdom
and encouragement.*

*To all the women who allowed their
stories of victory and pain to be shared in
this book to bring healing to many.*

By his wounds we are healed.

Isaiah 53:5

CONTENTS

WE'RE IN THIS TOGETHER

I woke up with my face smashed against a crushed glass windshield.

Is this real, or is it a dream? How did I get here?

Moments earlier I'd been watching my beautiful fifteen-year-old daughter sing in her first choir concert at church. Our family's moment of joy and excitement suddenly became our darkest moment.

On November 5, 2006, a drunk driver traveling more than eighty miles per hour struck our van head-on. In an instant, my husband, my two children, and I were physically broken, crushed in countless ways. We had no idea whether we would survive. My daughter, Jen, wasn't expected to live through the night because of traumatic brain injuries and multiple skull fractures. She remained in a coma for five weeks, and months passed before we were all reunited. Today our lives don't look like they once did, and they never will.

If you're reading this book, I suspect you've had a life-altering circumstance of your own. Maybe it was a divorce or a miscarriage. Perhaps you've experienced the death of a spouse or a child. Maybe you suffer from chronic pain, depression, or disease. My heart aches for you. Because of this circumstance, which you may or may not have chosen, your life will never be the same again. You might be feeling hopeless because you can no longer see the future you once imagined. You may still be in pain, wrestling with questions for which there are no answers. You may wonder if you deserve to be healed.

I get that.

What you may not realize is that if you haven't dealt with the wounds of your past, you'll carry that pain into your future. When your wounds remain buried, pain and infection spread. In the midst of your suffering, you end up hurting the ones you love most.

Perhaps you wonder if healing is really possible. Whether it's physical, emotional, or spiritual healing, we're all desperately searching for relief.

When you're brave enough to step into the broken places of your life, God promises to walk right beside you. Your escort is Jehovah Rapha, "the Lord your healer," who "takes hold of your right hand and says to you, Do not fear; I will help you" (Isa. 41:13).

Though I know it can feel scary to expose those tender places, this moment is your opportunity to experience more healing in your wounded heart. And because God helped me in my darkest days, I have hope for you today.

AN UNLIKELY SOURCE OF HEALING

In the years following our accident, as I lay in bed at night, I would pray for hours, begging God to come to my rescue and make me whole—physically, emotionally, and spiritually. When I cried out to God for more healing, He always brought me back to the cross, where Jesus suffered the most. Again and again, my mind pictured

God's innocent Son suffering and dying for me. When Jesus was betrayed, arrested, beaten, abandoned, falsely accused, mocked, judged, and tortured, He barely said a word.

As I begged God for healing, I started listening very carefully to the words Jesus spoke when He was in those final hours of suffering. Hanging on the cross, dying of suffocation, with barely enough oxygen to form a word, the weight of His whole body would have been crushing His diaphragm. The excruciating effort it took for Him to speak aloud quickened my ears to listen even more closely.

While we don't have access to Jesus's private prayers to His Father, He used every last ounce of strength to make seven final audible statements. Through the years my family has suffered, I've come to believe those words are one of Jesus's greatest gifts to our wounded souls. *Every single word He uttered on that cross carries life-giving power to heal our most painful places.*

Even though the cross is a one-time act of redemption, Jesus's final words have also become a crucial part of my *daily* healing. Through His work in my life, I've become convinced that because Jesus suffered on the cross, He understands my suffering and He understands yours.

The cross not only solves my sin problem by offering a future escape from this fallen world; it also solves my ongoing pain problem and gives me the power to live moment by moment amid the brokenness of our fallen world. Although there's a chronological order to what Jesus said on the cross, I've chosen to present these statements in the order they appear in the Gospels—Matthew, Mark, Luke, and John.

YOU'RE NOT ALONE

In the pages of this book, I'm going to share what God did to bring healing in my life. Then as we unpack the words of Jesus together, I'm going to walk you through a process that can help you find renewed hope for your life. I trust that Jesus has something beautiful in store for you as you courageously invite Him into your throbbing places.

By the time you put down this book, you'll be in the arms of Jesus. No matter what your experience has been or what your future holds, you'll know that Jesus cares and has a plan for you.

I'll be with you each step of the way, and Jesus will too.

My experience convinces me that God will use you in greater ways because of what you've been through. He often allows our wounds to change our destinies and the destinies of others. I've seen that so clearly through the life of my daughter, Jen. God not only heals our wounds, but He also turns our scars—the reminders of what we've endured—into beauty marks. And in God's unlikely kingdom economy, those beauty marks make us more fully who God created us to be than we'd be without them.

My prayer for you is that God would heal your heart a little more as you read this book and spend time with Jesus. God's Word is alive and powerful, and it can mend the broken places in your heart. Believing that "by his wounds we are healed" (Isa. 53:5), I'm asking God to do heart surgery on you (and me).

Because God is faithful, I'm convinced He wants to turn your scars into beauty marks and use you in ways you never dreamed possible.

Chapter 1

THE PHYSICIAN NO INSURANCE COMPANY CAN DENY

*Pain isn't the enemy. The inability or unwillingness
to face pain is a far greater danger.*

Samuel Chand, *Leadership Pain*

I have a scar. It runs from one eyebrow to the other. It's like my own permanent road map marking the shortest distance between one eyebrow and the other. My scar is evidence that I was wounded in the accident that changed my life forever. I should probably have plastic surgery to get it fixed once and for all. But when you've lived in the hospital for months, had multiple orthopedic surgeries, had a husband battling prostate cancer and a daughter with a traumatic brain injury, the last thing on your priority list is elective cosmetic surgery. So my scar remains.

Scars are evidence of wounds.

Though my left side was completely crushed, the scars no one saw were on my heart and in my soul. If you're like me and a lot of women I've met over the past few years, you may be living with internal scars as well.

Maybe it was something a father said or didn't say.

A betrayal by a friend.

A promise a spouse didn't keep.

A dream shattered by a boss or coach or spiritual leader you once admired.

A misunderstanding among neighbors or business partners.

Something unexpected.

Something unthinkable.

Something unspeakable.

Whether it happened yesterday or fifteen years ago, it still stings. You'd rather not revisit the source of that hurt, yet it left a mark on you that's impossible to erase. It resurfaces when you least expect it and flares up even though you try to suppress it, reminding you that you are no longer whole.

You were wounded.

Scars are reminders of the wounds we've endured. They trigger memories of the traumatic experiences we'd rather forget. We think scars are ugly. That's why we're driven to alter them, minimize them, or hide them. But even with all the Mederma cream in the world, they never *completely* fade.

The good news is that God longs to transform the scars on your wounded heart into marks of beauty. He can use them to bless the world. *Beauty marks are wounds that have been transformed into purpose.* They remind you that God is redeeming what you've suffered and can heal you from the inside out. Maybe your heart feels as if it's bleeding right now, and healing seems impossible. Trust that the God who created you and loves you is able to heal every broken place.

JESUS HAS SCARS TOO

The prophet Isaiah made this prediction about the Messiah:

> He was pierced for our transgressions,
> he was crushed for our iniquities;
> the punishment that brought us peace was on him,
> and by his wounds we are healed. (Isa. 53:5)

Scars mark the wounds that were inflicted on Jesus. On His hands. On His feet. On His side. On His head.

If you've read the story of the crucifixion, you know that the risen Jesus is probably covered from head to toe with scars from the beatings and the piercings He endured. The obvious scars were on His hands and His feet. But He had soul wounds too. His friends betrayed Him. His family abandoned Him. Religious leaders despised and rejected Him. He was forgotten. Forsaken. Falsely accused.

Yet when Jesus appeared to His followers after dying on the cross and rising from the dead, one of the first things He did, according to several gospel accounts, was to show them His scars. Isn't that interesting? He didn't try to hide them. In fact, it's as if Jesus was announcing, "You know it's *Me* because of these scars!" when He said, "Look at my hands and my feet. It is I myself!" (Luke 24:39).

Because I'm a woman with scars, I'm compelled to ask, Why does Jesus, the Son of God, still have scars? He is God Almighty in a resurrected, glorified body! I don't know about you, but I'm hoping to get rid of all of these scars when I get my new body in heaven. Though I don't know exactly what glorified bodies will look like, I do know that Jesus has "all authority in heaven and on earth" (Matt. 28:18), and I don't think He *had* to keep His scars. I think He *chose* to. His scars are evidence that He was wounded for us. His wounds heal our wounds. His scars are proof that we can be healed!

I think Jesus kept those scars to remind us that He loves us, that we are not alone, that we were worth all the pain and piercing. Every time we doubt, every time we have fears, every time we feel troubled or unworthy, we can look at the body of Jesus. Look at His hands! Look at His feet! Consider that these aren't merely scars. They are shouts of victory. Symbols of triumph. Statements of His unending love for us.

Jesus's scars became *beauty marks*. His suffering was transformed into purpose when He brought salvation to the world.

And those holy marks tell a story. Death could not stop Him. Sin could not keep Him in the grave. Sorrow could not tear Him apart. Jesus said, "In this world you will have trouble. But take heart! I have overcome the world" (John 16:33). He kept the scars to prove that because He was victorious, we can be too!

Jesus faced everything that threatens to hurt you—sorrow, sin, and death—and He was stronger still. He conquered them all for you. His love for you is written all over His body in scars. He chose not to erase, minimize, or hide them. He left them to remind you that every time you doubt, every time you fear, every time you hurt, you can be healed.

Sometimes, though, our healing doesn't come as quickly as we'd like.

I CAME TO JESUS. WHY DO I STILL HURT?

As a teen, Maria left home as soon as she could. Her father abandoned her before she was thirteen and never spoke to her again. At eighteen, she found love in the arms of an army man and married him. After serving two tours in Iraq and surviving a tank explosion that took the lives of his buddies, her husband came home with a traumatic brain injury and post-traumatic stress disorder (PTSD). Add to that stress a child with special needs and no family support, and Maria knew it was time to get help. She decided to go back to church.

She did everything they told her to do at church. She accepted Jesus as her Lord and Savior. She got baptized. She tried to pray. She volunteered. She joined a women's Bible study. But nothing seemed to make life any easier. On Sunday she would be encouraged, but by Monday her life would cycle back into chaos.

"I came to church because I thought my life would get better," Maria explained, "but instead, my guilt, pain, and hurt got worse. I felt like giving up. I could only assume that I wasn't good enough for God, like I wasn't good enough for my father."

Did God and the church overpromise and underdeliver in Maria's life? Can you relate to her story? Does the Christian life seem phony? Do you feel as if something is wrong with you? Do you think you need more faith? What do you do when your theology (what the Bible and the church say) doesn't match your reality (what your story says)?

The answers are found in understanding and walking in your new identity in Christ. Yes, God can heal you. No, you don't need more faith, but you do need to understand how God made you.

BEAUTIFULLY DESIGNED

God uniquely created each one of us to have a body, soul, and spirit. It helps me to think of these as *sense awareness* (body), *self-awareness* (soul), and *God awareness* (spirit). Jesus referred to all three in the garden of Gethsemane, right before He was taken captive to suffer and die on the cross. He cried out, "My soul is crushed with grief to the point of death.… The spirit is willing, but the body is weak!" (Matt. 26:38, 41 NLT). It has always been comforting to me to know that my Savior understands what it is to be a sense-aware, self-aware, God-aware person. Jesus surrendered to His Father's will, but it wasn't easy. What a great example for us to follow. When we're weak, we can run to the Father in prayer and tap into the power of the Holy Spirit, who lives in us.

I witnessed this in my daughter, Jen, when she emerged from a coma after her brain injury. Her mind, body, and emotions were broken. Yet the Holy Spirit was perfect and beautiful inside her. If you have accepted Jesus as your Savior, His Spirit is whole and perfect inside you too. None of us can escape the pain of this world. But we have the hope of heaven, where we will be completely healed one day with no more pain or suffering. Until that glorious day, understanding how God beautifully designed us influences how we understand our woundedness and His healing.

When we become believers in Christ, our spirits, which were dead, are regenerated and made alive in Christ and the Holy Spirit enters our hearts. However, our bodies and souls are still subject to temptation, decay, disease, and death in this fallen world. This is why a person can be genuinely born again in Christ and still have pain, problems, depression, addictions, and even sinful behaviors.

Because of our sin nature, we will never be completely whole until we get to heaven, but God longs to heal us a little more each day in our souls—our minds, wills, and emotions. He wants us to be whole. Unfortunately, lies from Satan, the enemy of our souls, attach to unhealed wounds, which can lead to unhealthy habits. If you feel as if a battle is going on in your soul for your mind, you're absolutely right! We still have our old ways of thinking. We have conscious thoughts—thinking and reasoning—and a lifetime of subconscious beliefs, attitudes, and memories we may not even be aware of. Soul wounds are usually caused by sin. Either someone sinned against us, or we sinned against ourselves. All of that damage takes time to undo.

God never intended for us to try to fix our broken, wounded souls ourselves. We can't fix them in our own strength. He gave us the power of *His Word* and *His Spirit* living in us to help us untangle the mess. Have you ever reached into your jewelry box to pull out a necklace and discovered that five of them were all tangled up together? I hate when that happens because it takes a long time to get the mess untangled. That's what our souls can feel like sometimes—a tangled-up mess!

Though it seems like a surprising prescription, the pain we've battled and resisted for so long can be our unlikely guide on this journey toward healing.

THE GIFT OF PAIN

My husband, Andy, has a history of prostate cancer in his family, but he hadn't had a checkup in years. He insisted he was feeling pretty good, so it was a miracle that I convinced him to go to the doctor to have blood work. When the results came back, we were shocked to find out that he had prostate cancer and needed immediate treatment. We almost caught it too late because Andy didn't have any pain. If we'd waited a month or two longer, the cancer could have breached the prostate and spread throughout his body. I'm typing this through tears because I'm so thankful for God's grace and mercy. I wish Andy had had some pain so that we could have discovered the cancer sooner. Pain tells us there's a problem. It's God's way of letting us know that something is wrong and it's time to take action. It's a warning sign to protect us from greater danger. A signal that it's time to do some deeper investigation.

Unfortunately, we can be tempted to think of pain as a punishment or a curse. After all, God promises no more pain or tears in heaven, so it would be easy to conclude that pain is bad. But what if we thought of pain as a gift? God knit the experience of pain into the fabric of humanity to give us warning signals, to keep us running back to Him, and to get us to admit that we need help. (That's why we won't need it any longer in heaven!) Pain leads us back to God's protective boundaries. Psalm 119:71 says it this way: "It was good for me to be afflicted so that I might learn your decrees." Nothing gets our attention quite like pain.

If you've ever gone to the doctor because you've been in pain, you know that the first step in any healing process is identifying what hurts and why. If we're to be healed, we have to get to the root of what's wrong. In essence, pain is the beginning of healing. Healing may not mean the pain goes away entirely. It may mean that it grows into a purpose. Either way, pain is a gift. It's meant to keep us from further harm. The problem is that we get so focused on pain as "a pain," we fail to see how it can actually help us.

I live with chronic pain. Maybe you do too. Each morning when I wake up and feel the nerve pain in my left hand and foot, I'm very aware of how much I need Jesus to get through the day. The truth is that the more pain I have, the more I talk to Jesus. Many days I pray, "Lord Jesus, please come to my rescue. Fill me with Your strength and courage today."

Pain is also what leads us to seek healing.

Our pain matters. It matters to God, and it matters to us.

Yet we can be tempted to manage our pain by minimizing it. We convince ourselves, *I can handle it. I'm fine. It will go away eventually.* If you were the oldest sibling in your family and one of your parents died, you might have had to bury your pain to hold the family together. If your husband's porn addiction or affair is crushing your heart, you might minimize your pain by reasoning that many marriages face the same challenges. Or you might minimize the loss of a father because your single mom did a great job raising you. But when you minimize your pain, you actually give it more power.

Sweet sister, ignoring pain is not strength. It leads to greater injury. Though our bodies have been exquisitely designed, our wounds need attention and care.

IDENTIFYING WOUNDS IN NEED OF HEALING

Like physical wounds, emotional wounds have symptoms. If you've been ignoring the signs or growing numb to your own pain, I'd like to share some tools to diagnose a soul wound. This is an opportunity for you to courageously identify what hurts. Pain isn't your enemy. It's your ally in finding the real problem.

Invite God to guide the process by praying these words:

Dear heavenly Father, please bring to my attention any wounds from my past or present that You are ready to start healing. Protect my heart and mind with the power of Your Holy Spirit as You guide me with Your gentle hand. Fill every broken place in my heart with Your truth. I trust You to heal me. In Jesus's name, amen.

Trusting God to guide you, look for clues that may signal unresolved wounds. I know this can be rough, but I promise, the good is coming. Here are ten symptoms that can help you identify wounds that need healing in your life:

1. You avoid specific places. You might avoid a former place of employment, a certain part of town, a house, or a ballpark. The place you avoid might even be church. Maybe religious leaders hurt or disappointed you. Jesus experienced this too.

If you avoid certain places because it hurts to go there, you have an unresolved wound. For example, I had a friend who would never let her children sleep overnight at our house. I didn't understand why until she explained that she was abused as a child during a sleepover at a friend's house.

2. You avoid certain people. Those "certain people" might be your family, which can be particularly difficult. They might be friends who betrayed you or people you fear will wound you again. If you imagine conversations about things you wish you had said to them but avoid engaging with them, you have an unresolved wound.

Several people I know avoid going home for Christmas because it causes them emotional pain to be around their fathers. It brings up wounds from their childhoods when they felt they weren't good enough or were unloved.

3. You have made a silent inner vow. Silent vows stem from unresolved wounds:

I will never let someone hurt me again.

I will never be like my mother.

I will never make my kids _____.

I will never trust a husband to provide for me.

I will never let _____ happen to my kids.

I met a precious woman who remarried after being a single mom for many years. She continued to keep her own separate bank account because of a vow she had made to never trust another man. One day God whispered to her heart, "You can trust your husband because you can trust Me." Not only did God mend her broken heart, but she also started to experience the blessing of a husband who wanted to provide for her.

4. You suffer from emotional triggers. You have painful memories connected to your five senses that are activated when you least expect them. Perhaps you experience an extreme emotional response when you hear a certain song, taste a certain drink, smell a certain fragrance, get touched in a certain place, or see a certain image. Another way of identifying triggers is by asking yourself, *What makes me angry? Fearful? Anxious? Embarrassed?*

A friend of mine said she couldn't figure out why she got so angry with her husband and children when they wasted food, until she finally realized that it triggered the pain of her father leaving her mom. They never had enough food to eat, so waste triggered her wound.

5. You engage in addictive behaviors or have an unhealthy attachment. Perhaps you have an addiction to food, exercise, alcohol, drugs, or work. Or you're in a codependent relationship with someone. Maybe you're always afraid that someone you love is going to walk out on you, hurt you, or disappoint you. If you struggle to feel confident in who you are, without anyone or anything else attached, you have an unresolved wound.

A friend in her midtwenties told me recently, "When I drink, I just go to sleep and I don't have to feel the pain. I don't have to face my fears."

6. You wound others. Hurting people hurt people. For example, if you tear down your husband and children with negative words or give them the silent treatment, you might be wounded. Perhaps you cut off friendships to protect yourself or rebel against parents or authority figures. If you have trouble respecting authority, you might have an unresolved wound.

A woman I pray with regularly was ready to leave her husband when God revealed to her that she had unhealed wounds and a deeply ingrained habit of rebelling against authority as a result of her mom leaving her as a teenager. When she allowed God to heal her past wounds, she was able to offer grace to her husband and submit to his authority as head of their family.

7. You experience ongoing, unresolved grief. If you have never grieved your losses—a loved one, a job, a marriage, or another deep loss—you have an unresolved wound. Maybe in the wake of your wounding, you went right back to work and kept doing the next thing on your calendar. At some point, you have to make time to process the grief, or you may face physical and emotional problems that force you to deal with it.

I have a friend who always wanted his wife right beside him. If they were walking with other couples and she fell behind to talk to someone, it would make him angry. Finally, after counseling, he realized that he had never fully grieved the unexpected death of his mother. Unknowingly, he struggled with the fear of losing someone he loved, and that led to control issues. Grief can rear its head decades after a loss.

8. Your thoughts bully you. You believe you're unworthy, unloved, useless, or disqualified. These thoughts can result in a poor self-image, isolation, shut-down emotions, or unrealistic expectations. But they are lies from Satan, the enemy of your soul. God's Word says you are loved, chosen, accepted, forgiven, and made new. Please don't make choices based on the lies you believe; instead, discover the truth of what God believes about you.

I met a sweet woman who grew up with an abusive, alcoholic father and then married an abusive husband. Because her thoughts bullied her, she believed the lie that she was unworthy of love and didn't deserve to be treated any better. She didn't realize that she was a priceless treasure, a daughter of the King.

9. You have a secret you've never told anyone. Perhaps you've rationalized that there's no need to share this secret with anyone. If it's a secret that doesn't involve you, then you may be right. But if it's a secret that's deeply affected you—even, and perhaps especially, a very old one—it might be time for that secret to come into the light. It's okay that you aren't okay. It's time to share your secret with someone you trust. It's not going away on its own.

A friend of mine wrote out her secret on notebook paper and showed it to her counselor. She said she felt so free and wondered why she had waited so long to deal with it. God had known her secret since she was a teenager and loved her anyway.

10. You struggle to verbalize your hurt. If you can't say "I am wounded" out loud without tears streaming down your face, you need healing. Enough said.

If you're experiencing any of these symptoms, you may be suffering from unresolved wounds from your past. Take a moment to grab a journal and list the symptoms you've noticed and prayerfully consider what might have caused the wounds you carry today. In the study guide, you'll be able to dig in to identify your symptoms and their causes.

Good Physician: Tell Jesus about your suffering and watch what He does with your wound. Begin and end your prayer by speaking hope aloud:

> He was despised and rejected by mankind,
> a man of suffering, and familiar with pain.
> Like one from whom people hide their faces.…
> Surely he took up our pain
> and bore our suffering. (Isa. 53:3–4)

Care: Now it's time to tell a safe person you trust about your wound, such as a pastor, mentor, counselor, or close friend. Whom could you tell? Ask that person to pray with you.

It's possible to be wounded even if others don't recognize your hurt. Deep down, you know it. You didn't need this book to dig it up.

Pause for a moment.

Now picture Jesus Himself holding your face in both of His nail-scarred hands and looking directly into your eyes. Hear Him say to you, *"I love you. I see you. I hear your cries. I remember you. I will take on your pain. I will heal you."*

Let those words soak into your soul!

Chapter 2

THE GREAT COVER-UP

Whatever is denied cannot be healed.

Brennan Manning, *Abba's Child*

"Linda, do you have any lotion?" my husband, Andy, asked. During our newlywed years, we owned a restaurant and Andy's hands were always dry and cracked from washing dishes.

"Oh, sure! I have one of those hotel samples in here somewhere," I answered while digging through my purse in the dark. We were winding through the backcountry roads near Hershey, Pennsylvania, on our way to Wednesday night church, and there wasn't a streetlight in sight.

After I found the lotion and handed it to him, Andy immediately started slathering it onto his hands.

Moments later he remarked, "Linda, this lotion isn't soaking into my skin."

"Keep trying. It's probably a cheap brand," I answered as he furiously tried rubbing the excess lotion from his hands onto his face and pants.

When we arrived at church, Andy dropped me off at the front door, and I slipped inside and into the back pew while he parked the car. A few moments later, he was sitting by my side.

"Linda, what happened to my pants?" he exclaimed. "You must have bleached my pants!"

I looked down to discover flesh-colored streaks all over his black pants. Then I looked up and saw his face. I could barely speak, I was laughing so hard.

In the dark I had accidentally handed him Mary Kay liquid cover-up, which he had smeared all over his hands, face, and pants, turning them all a nice shade of medium peach.

Many of us put on cover-up without knowing it. When Jen first came home from the hospital after our car wreck, I cried often, but as the years passed, I turned off the faucet of my emotions because I didn't want to hurt anymore. I just couldn't cope with the pain.

Maybe you can relate. Have you ever tried to cover up your wounded heart? Have you smiled at people and said you were fine when inside your heart was oozing pain and your mind was asking, *My God, my God, why have You forsaken me? Lord, I loved You with all my heart. Why didn't You protect my family? Why are we suffering?*

Sometimes when we grow up in church, we're tempted to cover up and pretend as if everything is fine. We're afraid to ask God hard questions because we don't want to be disappointed. We know He is able to relieve our suffering, but we have to trust that He will create beauty marks from our suffering and redeem all that the Enemy (Satan) has tried to steal from us.

After the accident, I kept convincing myself that I was fine. Everyone else thought I was fine. I was leading hundreds of women in Bible study every week. Certainly I had to be fine. But everything was far from fine.

SURVIVAL MODE

At first I was so physically injured from the car wreck, I was unaware of my emotional wounds. I was too busy hopping on one leg to the bathroom so I didn't have to use my wheelchair. I was trying to dress, bathe, and feed Jen with my one uninjured hand. Jen's brain injury was a global injury, and caring for her was a full-time job. She had so much physical pain. Every day she had severe migraines and pressure in her brain. Her body was hypersensitive, which meant she had pain every time she ate and every time someone touched her. I had to gently brush her arms, legs, hands, and feet every two hours to help her tolerate being touched. Several times a week we'd visit doctors and participate in therapy sessions. Emotional wounds were the last thing on my radar. It took me five years, when Jen and I finally had less physical pain, to uncover the emotional wounds and deal with them.

I wish I had run into God's arms sooner and admitted that I was a mess, but I kept right on doing the next thing, keeping busy encouraging others, taking care of Jen, tackling the next project—all so I didn't have to deal with my own pain. In fact, I had put up so many protective walls that I didn't even feel pain. I didn't feel anything. I was numb and dead inside. But the walls that kept me from feeling pain also kept me from feeling love or joy. I rarely cried, even when it was appropriate to cry. I was in survival mode.

I had to stay in survival mode to deal with my daughter's suffering. Jen would be crying in pain one minute and dancing for joy the next. She had cortical blindness, which meant she could see only out of certain parts of her eyes. Everything else was blocked. One doctor described it as looking through Swiss cheese. She would walk into doors and walls continually. Plus, she had stomach pain and threw up in the shower every day. I knew that if I took time to stop and process all that had happened to my family, I might fall into a deep, dark pit and never come out. I was alive, but I wasn't really living.

Finally I went to a counselor, and she reminded me that God made me in His image and that He has emotions too. He gets angry, He weeps, and He loves. The counselor explained that anger turned inward can lead to depression, and it was possible I'd been experiencing mild depression for several years.

She kept asking me, "How do you feel?"

I remember answering stoically, "What are my options?"

To face my feelings felt like more than I could manage. The counselor warned me that just as a covered pot of boiling water on the stove eventually erupts, my emotions would too.

"When you least expect it," she cautioned, "your emotions may explode, or you may have an anxiety attack."

SOMETHING SNAPPED

A few weeks later, I found myself sitting in driving school after getting two traffic tickets in a month. Bad month. If you've ever been to driving school, you know that the majority of the students are younger offenders, teenagers working off their first driving points. After a brief introduction, the teacher showed horrific videos of car crashes. Then he asked everyone to explain why they were attending.

One young man said, "I was going twenty-five miles over the speed limit."

A young lady replied, "I was drinking and driving."

A couple of other students started laughing and bragging about how officers had let them off easy and hadn't given them reckless-driving tickets. Rather than stopping the crude banter, the teacher coached them to dress up in nice clothes and suggested they plead guilty in court so the judge would be more lenient.

Suddenly something inside me snapped. Their apathy and laughter triggered all the feelings I'd struggled to identify in therapy.

I jumped up and started screaming, "This isn't a joke! You might kill someone! You can ruin a family's life. You can hurt a little girl. My daughter has a brain injury from an auto accident, and she will never be the same again!"

The beautiful blonde sitting behind me said, "Oh, hi, Mrs. Barrick. I used to play on the soccer team with Jen at school."

All of a sudden my heart felt as if it was pounding out of my chest, and I could hardly breathe. Jen had been a varsity soccer player, a varsity cheerleader, and a straight-A student. Yet in that one awful moment, everything had been taken from her. I started crying. Not the gentle kind that's easily masked. It was the loud, messy kind of crying. I'd held it all in until that moment because somewhere deep inside, I feared that if I ever started crying, I wouldn't be able to stop. Well, it happened to me that day. My protective walls cracked, and a flood of emotions came rushing out.

The teacher didn't know what to do with me.

Finally he said, "Ma'am, it's okay. You can go home now. You're here voluntarily, and I think you've earned your credit. Please, ma'am, go on safely home."

When I got into my car, I continued to weep. I have no idea how long I sat there. Finally I called my husband to come pick me up.

I never decided to let my wounds fester, but concealing had come easier than healing. I had no idea how big God's love really was until I began to open my heart and uncover my wounds. I went back to that counselor and started facing my hidden emotions. Slowly the walls that held my soul captive began to crumble.

Maybe, like me, you've kept your wounds covered up. You've fooled others and even fooled yourself. But God sees your cover-up. He's familiar with the inner turmoil in your heart. He's waiting for you to cry out to Him and ask, "My God, my God, why?" You might feel frightened, but if you're willing to uncover your wounds, God wants to heal you in ways you never dreamed possible.

DON'T BE AFRAID TO ASK WHY

In the first two accounts of the crucifixion, Matthew and Mark recorded only one statement Jesus spoke from the cross. It's a question that has to be answered before the healing process can begin: "My God, my God, why have you forsaken me?" (Matt. 27:46; Mark 15:34). Neither Matthew nor Mark was present at Jesus's crucifixion—all the disciples fled except John—so this statement may have been emphasized most often when eyewitnesses retold the story of Jesus's death.

This question is a direct quote from Psalm 22, a song King David wrote. It may have been easy to remember because it was familiar.

What we do know is what matters most: when the Son of God was in pain, He asked His Father, "Why?"

Jesus knew the heart and mind of God. He didn't need to ask why. In His deity, He could answer the question. But Jesus was also a man. He felt pain just as we do. And when He endured His greatest pain, when He hurt the most, He asked why.

By asking why, Jesus gave us permission to bring our tough questions to God. Because He asked why, we don't need to be ashamed of our own doubts and fears. God isn't angered because we need more answers. In fact, our tough questions may be the very thing that draws us closer to Him. The One who already knows our deepest inner thoughts and struggles offers us permission to share them with Him!

If you were standing before God right now, what would you ask Him?

Maybe you feel you're suffering because of someone else's sin. Or perhaps you feel as if you're being punished or you've been forgotten. Ask God. He wants to have a two-way conversation with you. Talk to Him aloud or write down your questions in a journal and listen to what He whispers to your heart. God can also speak to you through His Word. Open up your Bible and read God's love letter to you. If you need help navigating the Scriptures, visit www.biblegateway.com and type in a keyword, such as *hope, fear, joy, peace,* or *healing,* to discover some of the verses in the Bible that contain those words.

By asking why, Jesus validated our natural need for our suffering to be seen and heard. Even though I believe pain has a purpose, I dream of heaven, where there will be no more pain or suffering. We don't have to pretend to be stronger than we are or mask our true feelings and longings. Jesus felt emotions, and we can too.

By asking why, Jesus modeled what we can do with our pain. When we're wounded, we can tell someone. Our Enemy tempts us to keep our pain hidden in the dark because he lives in darkness. Satan controls what we keep hidden in darkness, but *when we bring our wounds into the light, Satan no longer has power over them.* Jesus is the light! When we acknowledge our pain, He begins to heal us.

If you've ever watched a wound-care specialist treat a wound, you know that the first thing he or she does is uncover the wound. It's briefly exposed to clean it out with disinfectant and get rid of the germs. The worst thing to do for a wound is to keep it covered up and allow infection to fester. I hate the sight of blood as much as anyone, and I've seen enough of it to last a lifetime, but I do marvel at God's design to rid our bodies of infection. White blood cells can help fight infection and bring oxygen and nutrients to the wound. Bleeding, or releasing what is hurting, is essential for both physical and emotional healing.

STACEY'S STORY

Stacey kept her secret for nearly twenty-five years. When a painful memory was triggered, she would push the thought or feeling away and focus on something else. First she threw herself into sports, and then boys, exercising, marriage, and parenting. But she could never get away from feeling as if she wasn't good enough.

"I felt so unloved," she shared with me. "I remember thinking if people knew how dirty I was, they wouldn't want me. They wouldn't want me in their church. They wouldn't want me in their

Bible study. My husband wouldn't want to stay married to me." Then she added, "I was constantly trying to make my story go away."

Stacey's secret began when she was seven. Seven is too young to process the pain of a broken toy, so imagine trying to process the pain of being sexually abused by your brother's best friend only a few feet from the safety of your mother. For three years a trusted neighbor molested Stacey in her own home and her own yard. Though she never verbalized her confusion, she wondered, *Why did God let this happen? Why didn't my mother protect me?* Stacey's natural defense—blocking her memory of the experience—is common among traumatized children.

Can you relate to Stacey? Have you ever tried to hide or cover up painful memories? I have. Even though revealing our wounds is painful, the benefit is worth it. God can mend our broken hearts one stitch at a time when we're willing to admit we have a problem.

When Stacey's son was young, she knew she never wanted him to bear the kind of secret she carried. It's what finally got her through the door to see a counselor.

"The day I finally decided to say the words *I was abused*, the knotted-up pain in my heart exploded. It was like the floodgates opened. Pain rushed out, and Jesus rushed in. I don't know that the pain will ever be completely gone, but since I made space for Christ to begin healing me, it doesn't consume me anymore like it did for so many years."

Stacey was finally willing to uncover her wound so her son would never have to nurse a wound alone. Your Savior, Jesus, exposed His wounded heart on the cross so you would know that you are never alone in your pain. Isaiah 53:3 tells us that "he was despised and rejected by mankind, a man of suffering, and familiar with pain." Your Savior understands what pain feels like. In His final moments, He showed you that it's okay to face your pain.

START WITH GOD

It's not enough to ask why; we have to ask *God* why. The key to Jesus's question on the cross is that He started with God: "My God, my God, why?" When we ask why apart from God, shame and blame rush in.

Anytime shame is attached to the answer you hear, it isn't from God. If you ask God why—"Why did my father abandon me?" "Why did my husband leave me?"—and you hear shame—"You weren't good enough." "You weren't worthy of love." "You were too much to handle."—that isn't God's voice. Shame always bears the signature of the Enemy.

Guilt is feeling bad about poor decisions you make; shame is feeling bad about who you are. Shame is a toxic disease that prevents you from accessing help and healing. But you can defeat shame with the truth of what God believes about you.

Shame Says	God Says
You aren't worth anything.	You are worth dying for.
You aren't good enough.	You are fearfully and wonderfully made.
You deserve to pay for your sin.	You are so loved, Jesus made the payment for you.

Refuse to allow shame to fester. When the lies of shame attach to your wound, they drag you into a deeper pit and tempt you to sin. But you can counteract shame when you offer your whys to God.

PROCESSING YOUR EMOTIONS

Asking why is a vulnerable act. When you're willing, God will teach you when, where, and how to be transparent with Him and others. Here are a few suggestions:

Pray to God. Ask God your questions aloud. Curl up in your favorite chair or get on your knees and pour out your heart to Him. Start by speaking Jesus's words from the cross: "My God, my God, why have you forsaken me?" (Matt. 27:46).

You can also pray by writing a letter to God. Tell Him all your feelings and ask Him all your questions. Don't sugarcoat any of it! God already knows your thoughts. He wants you to bring your mess to Him so He can begin to mend your wounded heart.

Open up with a professional. Talk to a Christian counselor or psychologist. Emotions give you good information, but they are not always an accurate reflection of reality. A counselor will guide you.

Meet with your pastor or a spiritual leader. Though a pastor or spiritual leader might not have the same experience as a professional counselor, he or she can point you to truth from God's Word and pray with you.

Share with trusted Christians. Tell the members of your Bible study or small group what you're facing so they can cover you in prayer, help meet your needs, and offer accountability.

Speak your emotions aloud. Try empty-chair therapy. This technique can be very helpful, particularly in cases where death, separation, or illness prevents you from talking to the person who wounded you. Basically, you say aloud to an empty chair everything you wish you could say to the person who hurt you. In other words, go somewhere no one can hear you and scream!

My counselor once wisely advised, "Linda, don't let your emotions control you. It's okay to choose when to open your heart and when to guard it." She encouraged me to imagine placing my wounds in a box and putting that box on my mantel. I can see it. I know it's there. Anytime I need to, I can take that box down and open it up with God. I can pray honest prayers as I cry and let Him hold me in His arms. But I can also choose to close it up and take a break from the pain.

You need to open your heart and uncover your wound, but you don't have to leave it open for everyone to access. Just as a wound-care specialist opens a wound, cleans it out, and wraps it back up, you can limit and control how much you reveal to others.

HAVE YOU FORSAKEN ME?

After hanging on the cross for six hours, three of those hours in total darkness, Jesus cried out to His Father, "*Eli, Eli, lema sabachthani?*"—"My God, my God, why have you forsaken me?" (Matt. 27:45–46; see also Mark 15:34).

Every other time Jesus spoke to God, He called Him Father. But this time, He addressed His Father as God. The intimacy in their relationship had shifted.

When the sins of the world were poured out on God the Son, God the Father could no longer look on Him with favor. Jesus felt the wrath of God against our sins and cried out, "Why have you forsaken me?"

Jesus felt utterly alone.

Was Jesus separated from God? Did the Trinity splinter? To say that God abandoned Jesus would be like saying that God could somehow abandon God or that Jesus ceased to be God. In His deity, Jesus couldn't become separated from God. But in His humanity, Jesus felt forsaken.

He was forsaken in the sense that no one came to His rescue. When He took the penalty for our sin, no one stopped Him. No one removed that filth. He had to carry it alone.

NOTHING CAN SEPARATE YOU FROM GOD'S LOVE

Do you know that Jesus was forsaken so that you would never have to be? His promise to you is that He will never leave you or forsake you (see Heb. 13:5). He took your punishment so you will never have to experience the wrath of God. Once you've accepted His forgiveness for your sins, there is nothing you can ever do to make God look on you with shame or anything other than favor! Your Father looked in judgment and disgust on your sin when Jesus took care of it once and for all on the cross. It has been paid for. You may *feel* separated from God, but once you are His child, you cannot *be* separated from Him. Nothing can ever separate you from His love! Romans 8:38–39 says, "I am convinced that neither death nor life, neither angels nor demons, neither the present nor the future, nor any powers, neither height nor depth, nor anything else in all creation, will be able to separate us from the love of God that is in Christ Jesus our Lord."

Nothing! You can finally lay your shame down.

EXPOSE THE LIES

When I speak, I often ask women to write down their wounds on note cards. And on the back, they identify the lies they have believed because of those wounds. My daughter and I pray over the thousands of note cards from women ages twelve to eighty-two.

One day I spread all the cards out on my dining-room table. I was going to take a picture of them when I noticed something important—while the wounds were very different, at the root of every lie was *shame*:

- No one loves me.
- I'm unworthy.
- I'm unforgiven.
- I'm not good enough.
- I'm not beautiful.
- I'm invisible.
- I'm worthless.
- I'm not smart enough.
- I can't trust anyone.
- I'm useless.

Have you ever believed any of those lies? Does it give you hope to know you're not alone?

The Enemy is using the same lies on all of us and getting away with it. In John 8:44, Satan, the Devil, is called the "father of lies." If he can keep us thinking we're the only ones who are unloved, unworthy, invisible, unforgiven, worthless, not good enough, or not beautiful, he wins. But when we expose his scheme, the power of shame is weakened.

I know you might feel alone. As if you're the only one who carries your kind of shame. But dear one, you no longer need to bear that shame, because Jesus has already carried it for you.

My daughter, Jen, one of the most amazing spiritual warriors I've ever met, uses the weapon of prayer against Satan's lies. When she can't remember something and is tempted to believe the lie that she isn't smart enough, she'll say out loud, "Satan, the only power you have over me is the power I give you by the lies I choose to believe. I'm believing God's Word that says I can do all things through Christ who strengthens me!"

The next time you're tempted to believe a lie about yourself, try speaking Jen's words aloud. I've done it many times, and it is one of the quickest ways to get Satan to flee.

BECKY'S STORY

During her childhood, Becky's father abandoned her, and her mother neglected her. As an adult, Becky married an alcoholic with PTSD. Thankfully she connected with a group of believers who gave her grace and taught her the truth about how God viewed her. But there was one wound she was most ashamed of and never shared with anyone: her abortion.

Becky's mother had told her that if she ever got pregnant, she would disown her. To a girl whose father had already abandoned her, that was a serious threat. So Becky chose to abort her baby.

It was the one wound she couldn't talk about. Maybe it was because the others happened to her but this one she chose. Maybe it was because she feared God could forgive her of everything else, but not this. Becky led a Bible study and helped other women find healing, but she kept this one wound buried—until she gave birth to her daughter.

Seeing that beautiful, innocent baby ripped Becky's wound wide open. She couldn't stop crying. She couldn't sleep because of the guilt. She tried reading Scripture and praying, but nothing seemed to help.

One day at her Bible study, she decided to tell her story. Her whole story. She finally talked about her abortion and the shame she'd endured eight years. Becky was still so ashamed that, initially, sharing made her feel worse instead of better.

But then a woman about two decades older, who was sitting across the table from Becky, bravely offered two words that God used to help set Becky free: "Me too."

This woman shared with the group that she'd also had an abortion during her teenage years.

There is so much power and healing in the words *Me too*. Ladies, you are not alone. Others have experienced something similar to what you've experienced. Your Enemy's tired trick is to repackage the same accusations and make you think you're the only one.

It's why your Savior fought for the breath to shout to you from the cross, "Me too! I have felt forsaken by God too. I have wondered why too." He didn't fight to get those words out so that you would carry your shame alone. It's time for you to tell someone. It's time for you to uncover your wound and write a letter to God or ask aloud, "My God, my God, why have You forsaken me?"

Now that you've identified your wound out loud, how do you exchange the bitterness for freedom?

Chapter 3

DEAR GRANT ...

The voice of sin may be loud, but the voice of forgiveness is louder.
Dwight L. Moody, *Prevailing Prayer*

"We have the results of the biopsy. I'm so sorry ... it's cancer."

Even the doctor cried as she told me. These are words you never want to hear. They shot a hole straight through my gut, not because she was referring to me but because she was talking about my twenty-two-year-old daughter. Jen had already been through so much at her young age. She had a brain injury she didn't deserve, and now cancer?

Lord, what in the world? Why?

As a mom, my heart was breaking. I walked out of the doctor's office alone. I couldn't show a hint of emotion on my face. Andy and Jen were sitting in the waiting room, and I didn't want her to know that she had thyroid cancer until I discussed it with Andy. Inside, I was crumbling all over again. We learned that her cancer probably resulted from all the CT scans she had on her head after her brain injury. Once again, my innocent daughter was suffering because of the sin of someone else.

I thought I had forgiven the drunk driver who hit us. I thought I had forgiven the negligent police officer who could have prevented the accident. I thought I had forgiven the insurance company that kicked us out of the rehab hospital. I thought I had stopped blaming God, who could have kept it all from happening in the first place. But when I heard Jen's diagnosis, all the bitterness came rushing back. I was so angry! I didn't tell anyone because I was trying to be strong for Jen, but I was wrestling mightily with God in my heart and mind.

Why, Lord? If You are all-powerful and if You are good, why would You let Jen suffer again?

As I struggled with God, He showed me that just as Jen's cancer was a toxin we had to get out so it didn't kill her, bitterness was also a toxin. A cancer of the soul. And it was spreading inside me. I could ignore it for a while, but sooner or later, I'd have to remove it, or it would torment my soul. In the following months, God equipped me to forgive all over again, but at a much deeper level.

Forgiveness is like cleaning out a wound. Just as physical wounds often have layers of tissue that need to be cleaned out daily to prevent infection, emotional wounds can also have layers that require us to forgive again and again. Forgiveness is rarely a once-and-done breakthrough. (Wouldn't that be nice?) It's more like a habit one develops over time. Forgiveness itself doesn't heal our wounds; only God can do that. *Forgiveness sets us free from the bitterness that infects our wounds and positions us so that God can make us whole.* In that sense, forgiveness is necessary for our healing to continue.

WHAT FORGIVENESS IS AND IS NOT

Sometimes understanding what something is requires that we first understand what it is not. To see if you truly understand forgiveness, read the following statements and respond "True" or "False."

1. People shouldn't be forgiven until they're truly sorry for their actions.
2. A person cannot genuinely forgive if he or she still feels hurt or angry.
3. Forgiveness involves fully restoring the offender.
4. A person hasn't really forgiven until he or she has forgotten the offense.
5. Forgiveness cancels the offender's consequences.

Do you feel conflicted about a few of your answers? Depending on your experiences, you may have found it difficult to choose between "True" and "False." But forgiveness isn't a black-or-white issue. It might surprise you to learn that according to Jesus's example, the answer to every single statement is "False."

In the midst of suffering on the cross, while soldiers were mocking and abusing Him, Jesus responded in a way that may be hard for us to comprehend:

> Two other men, both criminals, were also led out with [Jesus] to be executed. When they came to the place called the Skull, they crucified him there, along with the criminals—one on his right, the other on his left. Jesus said, "Father, forgive them, for they do not know what they are doing." And they divided up his clothes by casting lots.

The people stood watching, and the rulers even sneered at him....

The soldiers also came up and mocked him....

One of the criminals who hung there hurled insults at him. (Luke 23:32–36, 39)

On the cross, Jesus showed us what forgiveness can look like in our lives every day. Let's examine each true/false statement from His perspective:

1. People shouldn't be forgiven until they're truly sorry for their actions. (False.) Forgiveness isn't conditional. (I'm not talking about trusting them or having a relationship with them. I'm talking about getting rid of your bitterness so it doesn't torture you and consume you any longer.) If you're waiting for the person who wounded you to say "I'm sorry," you aren't really forgiving; you're bargaining. If you're thinking, *I'll forgive when this person asks for my forgiveness*, you're taking a gamble. Your offender may not ever ask for forgiveness. The person may not even realize how much he or she has hurt you. Do you really want to gamble while bitterness grows in your soul? Forgiveness is within your control. It's your choice. You may have done nothing to deserve your pain, but you can do something about healing it.

Jesus didn't deserve the pain of the cross. No one was asking for His forgiveness when He graciously said, "Father, forgive them." In fact, His offenders went right on casting lots for His garments, mocking Him, and insulting Him. They didn't seem to hear Jesus, and they certainly didn't have a change of heart about their actions. You might go out on a limb to offer forgiveness and get absolutely no response from your offender. That's okay. Forgiveness isn't contingent on the offender or the offense, but it will lubricate the healing of your heart.

2. A person cannot genuinely forgive if he or she still feels hurt or angry. (False.) Forgiveness isn't the absence of pain, anger, or hurt. After Jesus extended forgiveness, He still shouted out in pain, "My God, my God, why have you forsaken me?" Your heavenly Father doesn't dismiss your pain. He sent His Son to the cross to shoulder it. Similarly, forgiveness doesn't require that you endorse abuse, unfaithfulness, divorce, theft, or any other sin committed against you. Anger and pain are God-given emotions that tell us something is wrong and action needs to be taken. Your heavenly Father doesn't frown upon your anger. He also feels angry over injustice and needless suffering.

Forgiveness isn't a feeling; it's an action. It was love that moved God to action (forgiveness) and caused Him to send a savior into our world of pain: "For God so loved the world that he gave his one and only Son, that whoever believes in him shall not perish but have eternal life" (John 3:16).

3. Forgiveness involves fully restoring the offender. (False.) Forgiveness isn't the same as restoration or restitution. It's possible to forgive even if a relationship isn't fully restored. In fact, in some circumstances, you may never have the opportunity to tell your offender that he or she wounded you or that you've granted forgiveness. The soldiers who crucified Jesus never made restitution for the harm they did. Jesus could only recognize that they didn't know what they were doing. But that didn't stop Him from forgiving them.

While restoration is often the goal of forgiveness, it isn't always possible. Your offender may have passed away or may be unwilling to reconcile your relationship. Or it may be unsafe or unwise for you to continue your relationship. For example, a woman who forgives an abusive husband may still need to move out of the house and establish safe boundaries. An employer who forgives a dishonest employee may still need to take away the keys and change the locks. Forgiveness doesn't mean agreeing to endure further abuse. Complete forgiveness doesn't depend on complete restoration.

4. A person hasn't really forgiven until he or she has forgotten the offense. (False.) Forgiveness isn't forgetting. The forgive-and-forget theory has one giant flaw: it's not humanly possible! We may forget many things—names, grocery lists, phone numbers, math facts—but painful experiences usually aren't among them. God wired our brains to hold on to things that hurt us. We might bury them for a while, but eventually they resurface. Jesus, who chose to keep the scars on His hands and feet, didn't seem compelled to forget the cross. Yet He forgave the ones who put Him there.

When we choose forgiveness, we're no longer consumed with thoughts about the person who hurt us. Feelings of hatred and bitterness no longer control us. When we forgive, our pain is transformed into a beauty mark, evidence that God is healing our wounds for a greater purpose.

Pastor Rick Warren explained it best when he said, "There's something better than forgiving and forgetting.… [It's] forgiving and then remembering the hurt and seeing how God can bring good out of it. That's more important than forgetting … because then you thank God for it.… You don't thank God for things you forget."[1]

5. Forgiveness cancels the offender's consequences. (False.) Forgiveness isn't the absence of consequences. If forgiveness canceled consequences, Jesus would never have had to die on the cross.

Because mercy and justice coexist in God's nature, somebody had to pay the penalty for sin. Conversely, allowing consequences doesn't mean you are unforgiving. In other words, you can forgive your teenager for lying and still take away his cell phone. You can forgive an employee for stealing and still release her from her job. You can forgive an abusive father or husband, but he still needs to face the legal consequences of his actions.

Both forgiveness and consequences come from God. All the way back to the garden of Eden, God is both the one who forgives and the one who disciplines. Because He is the author of forgiveness, we can forgive. Because He is the author of consequences, we can trust Him to administer justice. My daughter, Jen, says it like this: "Take people off your hook and put them on God's hook. Then you will be free!"

DON'T LET BITTERNESS TAKE ROOT

While they were still driving the nails into His hands and hurling insults at Him, Jesus was praying, "Father, forgive them." He refused to let any bitterness take root. I suspect He was teaching us that the sooner we forgive, the better. Once the bitterness takes root, it's much harder to dig it up.

For most of us, forgiveness is a process.

Maybe someone who was supposed to protect you and keep you safe hurt you. Abused you. Destroyed your security. You might be thinking, *It's impossible to forgive.* You're right! I don't think we can forgive in our own strength. We need to ask God our Father to help us.

We may think we're too hurt to forgive, but we may be hurting ourselves more by not forgiving. What if you and I could say "Father, forgive them" as soon as we're wounded? Would you be willing to try it? Next time someone hurts you, let the first words out of your mouth be "Father, forgive them." What if it became a habit? What if it became your go-to coping mechanism? Even if you have to say it twenty times a day, I challenge you to try it. Notice what it does for your heart.

"THEY DO NOT KNOW WHAT THEY ARE DOING"

After interviewing hundreds of wounded women, I've discovered that what helps them forgive is echoed in the statement Jesus made about His offenders: "They do not know what they are doing" (Luke 23:34). The soldiers didn't know who He was. They had to do their job, or they could have lost their lives. The religious leaders didn't recognize Jesus as the Messiah. They didn't know they were crucifying the One who came to save them.

Though it's not always easy, finding a way to empathize with the pain or problems of the offender can help us forgive when we've been wounded. Stepping into the shoes of the offender can breed that kind of understanding and compassion.

My friend's abusive father abandoned her before she was a teenager. She expressed how impossible it was to forgive him: "Someone who was supposed to protect me and love me destroyed me." After many years of counseling, the one thing that has helped her forgive is picturing how wounded and broken her father was as a boy. She finally realized he wasn't capable of giving love he never received.

When I put myself in the shoes of the drunk driver who hit us, I can recognize that he was filling his life with drugs and alcohol to medicate the pain of this world. Without Jesus, I might be tempted to do the same thing.

As Anne Graham Lotz observed, "The wounded become wounders."[2] If you're hurting others, you've most likely been hurt yourself. Identifying a wound in others doesn't justify their actions, but it can make it a little easier to forgive. It's like the thief who steals food because he's starving. Understanding that he stole because he was starving doesn't make the wrong right, but it explains why he did it and ignites our compassion.

Maybe the person who wounded you was incapable of giving the love or attention you needed because he (or she) was once a victim. Perhaps he really had no idea how much pain his actions would cause you. Maybe he was too broken to make sense of his own mess, much less save you from yours. By noticing painful wounds in the person who hurt you, you might discover that he was never capable of anything more.

The common denominator in the women I interviewed who felt empathy for their offenders was that the pain attached to their wounds no longer had power over them.

ELAINE'S STORY

When Elaine was growing up, her father and his parents lived fewer than ten miles from her yet never acknowledged her existence. Elaine had been the result of an unexpected teenage pregnancy, and her father's legalistic family dealt with it by ignoring her. Elaine's paternal grandmother was the pillar of their little country church but never admitted publicly that she had a granddaughter. She did, however, name Elaine in her will, but only to legally disown her so she would never be able to inherit a single thing from her.

For a while, Elaine shared her grandmother's unforgiving spirit, blaming her absent alcoholic father for her own mistakes. For years Elaine was angry with the mystery father who never came to watch her play sports at school, cared enough to send a birthday card, or walked her down the aisle when she married. Then at age thirty-eight, Elaine found Jesus. Not the god of religion, but the God of grace and truth. When she discovered genuine forgiveness, she knew she needed to forgive her earthly father as her heavenly Father had forgiven her.

There was one problem. Her father was no longer living. His absence had ruined half of her life while he was living, and now it threatened to ruin the other half because he was dead and restoration was impossible. She went to his grave anyway. She had planned to execute a version of empty-chair therapy by confessing to the headstone everything she had ever blamed her father for and all the hurt he had caused her. She had planned to empty her soul of pain. But when she stood beside his grave, she realized that at the time of his death, her father had been five years younger than she was now. Suddenly she felt sorry for him. His mistakes had cut his own life short. When she began to see him as a lost, hurting soul and realized that he was probably more wounded than she, her bitterness melted away.

For the first time in her life, she thought about how painful it must have been for him to grow up in a family that had no room for grace. With tears streaming down her face, Elaine dropped to her knees and whispered, "Daddy, I don't hate you anymore. I forgive you."

Once you receive God's forgiveness, He *commands* you to forgive others. It's nearly impossible to forgive unless you've been forgiven. How can you pass on something that you haven't experienced yourself? How can you give away something that isn't already yours? Forgiveness requires divine strength that comes from having first received grace yourself. Ephesians 4:32 charges us to "be kind and compassionate to one another, forgiving each other, just as in Christ God forgave you." The ability to fully forgive others comes after God has forgiven you.

If you've never known what it feels like to have God Almighty remove the shame and weight of every dark, ugly sin "as far as the east is from the west" (Ps. 103:12), you might need to receive His forgiveness. If you aren't certain that one day the God of heaven will be waiting with open arms to welcome you into His presence as His child, no matter where you've been or what you've done, all you have to do is ask, "Father, forgive me." If forgiving others feels impossible right now, start with your own heart.

Jesus taught His disciples about forgiveness when He taught them how to pray, "Forgive us our debts, as we also have forgiven our debtors" (Matt. 6:12). Then He went a step further, saying, "But if you refuse to forgive others, your Father will not forgive your sins" (Matt. 6:15 NLT).

Ouch! Did Jesus mean that He'll take our forgiveness back if we don't forgive someone else? If you read this passage alongside all the other verses on forgiveness in the Bible, I think He meant two things. First, forgiveness isn't optional. God doesn't suggest that we forgive; it's a command. Second, forgiveness is for our benefit. *Our intimacy with God is hindered when we don't forgive.*

God's commands are always for our good, not our harm. God knows that forgiveness will improve our mental and physical well-being. In fact, according to the Mayo Clinic, forgiveness has many benefits, including better relationships, decreased anxiety and stress, lower blood pressure, fewer symptoms of depression, a stronger immune system, and a healthier heart.[3] When we hold on to bitterness, we're poisoning ourselves!

I know how hard it is to forgive, but we cannot receive the amazing grace of God and not extend forgiveness to others. If I can't forgive my husband, then I'm holding something against him that Jesus has already paid for. In essence, I'm saying, "Jesus, Your payment wasn't good enough." And if Jesus's payment wasn't good enough to cover my husband's sin against me, then how could His payment be good enough to cover my own sin? It doesn't make sense to ask someone to keep paying for something that's already been paid for.

Close relatives of mine leased an SUV during their car-seat season of life. At the end of the lease, they turned in the vehicle to the dealership, but the dealership failed to report it to the corporate office. For months my relatives received threatening letters from the corporate office demanding that they return the vehicle or pay a penalty plus the cost of the vehicle. They kept trying to explain that they had already returned the vehicle. Finally the paperwork got cleared up, and they got a statement that said, "We're sorry. We discovered that all this time your debt had been paid in full." The same thing is true for the people who have wronged you. Jesus paid their debt in full on the cross. There is nothing left for you to collect from them.

FORGIVE YOURSELF

The same is true for you: Jesus paid your debt in full on the cross. If you're struggling to forgive yourself for something, remember that God has already cleared your record. Your Enemy, Satan, wants you to keep condemning yourself for the sins Jesus already paid for on the cross. You are no longer a slave to the sin God has forgiven. Ask Him to help you stop blaming and condemning yourself so you can be set free.

There are no verses in the Bible that say you have to forgive yourself. Instead, we're invited to accept God's redemptive grace. I love the promise in 1 John 1:9: "If we confess our sins, he is faithful and just and will forgive us our sins and purify us from all unrighteousness." Satan is the one who keeps filling us with lies that we're unworthy and unforgiven. He is a liar and the enemy of our souls. The next time you feel unworthy or unforgiven, say out loud, "Satan, you are a liar! I have been forgiven for _____. I've been washed clean by the blood of Jesus!"

Forgiveness fosters freedom.

CHOOSE FORGIVENESS EVERY DAY

Maybe you don't want to forgive the person who hurt you. I understand. Forgiveness isn't a feeling; it's a choice you make every day. There are a few practical guidelines that help me break free from my bitterness when I'm stuck in unforgiveness.

Recognize the real enemy. Satan is the real enemy, not the person who hurt you. Satan is the one who wants to destroy your family, your marriage, and your emotional well-being. If you want to blame someone, blame him. The apostle Peter exhorted us to "be alert and of sober mind. Your enemy the devil prowls around like a roaring lion looking for someone to devour" (1 Pet. 5:8). Paul concurred: "For we are not fighting against flesh-and-blood enemies, but against evil rulers and authorities of the unseen world, against mighty powers in this dark world, and against evil spirits in the heavenly places" (Eph. 6:12 NLT).

Pray for the person who hurt you. You can't stay bitter toward someone you're praying for, even if all you can say is "Father, forgive them, for they do not know what they are doing." I really believe when I started praying these words of Jesus, my bitterness and blame began to shrink. As you pray for the person who harmed you, God will help you respond to evil with good.

Ask God to redeem everything the Enemy has tried to steal from you. God is the only one who can repay what was taken from you. Your offender can't really fix the harm that was done. And vengeance won't either. But God can heal your heart and restore a hundred times over what you've lost. Deuteronomy 30:3 promises that "GOD, your God, will restore everything you lost; he'll have compassion on you; he'll come back and pick up the pieces from all the places where you were scattered" (THE MESSAGE). Instead of focusing on the hurt, notice the emerging beauty mark, a reminder that God is transforming your wound into a purpose that is far greater than your pain.

UNLIKELY FORGIVENESS

While I was still wrestling with God over Jen having thyroid cancer, she marched into the family room and announced that He was telling her to write a letter to the man who hit us, telling him she had forgiven him. At that time, he was still in a vegetative state, but Jen thought maybe the letter would help his family heal in new ways. She was eager to see what God would do. Here is what she wrote with God's help:

Dear Grant,

My name is Jennifer Barrick. I don't know if you know who I am, but I am a twenty-two-year-old girl who prays for you every day. I am asking God to heal you so that you can talk and walk again! One day I hope to meet you and pray over you in person, but more importantly, I want to meet you in heaven one day—where there is no more pain and no more tears.

I have a brain injury because you were drinking and driving, and I have suffered a lot too. I like to think that God remolded me and made me better. Even though I have disabilities and struggle every day, God is using me in ways I never dreamed possible for His glory.

I want you to know that I have forgiven you—not in my own strength, but in God's strength. I can't explain it, but God has given me a special love for you. I will continue to pray for you daily.

Love,

Jen

How in the world could my brain-injured daughter living with cancer come up with those words? The only explanation is that the Spirit of God is alive and strong in her. I didn't teach her those things. God taught them to her, and she taught them to me.

The most amazing thing has happened over the past few years since Jen sent that forgiveness letter. Her healing has progressed faster than ever. Not only that, but God has been healing the drunk driver in new ways as well. Doctors removed his feeding tube, and he's now able to eat by mouth. He's also beginning to communicate. I don't know what God is up to or how the story will end, but I do know that forgiveness is the catalyst for healing in the hearts of both victims and offenders, wounded sons and daughters, in equal need of a savior.

Jen has written a prayer you can use when you pray for someone who has hurt you:

> *Dear heavenly Father,*
>
> *Please heal _____ beyond what is humanly possible so that he/she can understand more about Your love and grace. May _____ hear Your voice and come to know You as his/her personal Lord and Savior. Today I choose to forgive _____ as You forgave me. Thank You for second chances.*
>
> *Lord, please take away _____'s pain and cradle him/ her in Your everlasting arms. I know that You can whisper hope to _____ as You did to me. Nothing is too hard for You.*
>
> *In Jesus's name. Amen.*

Would you be willing, with God's help, to pray this prayer, filling in the blanks with the name of the person who wounded you? When you clean out your wound by forgiving, God can turn your pain into purpose.

Chapter 4

WHAT DOES PAIN HAVE TO DO WITH PARADISE?

Sometimes God permits what He hates to accomplish that which He loves.

Joni Eareckson Tada, quoting her friend Steve

As I looked around the cancer center, I sighed. "Oh, Jen, you're the youngest one here."

Jen exclaimed loudly, "Yes, but I know the Healer!"

The receptionist chimed in, "You preach it, girl!"

Jen had already decided that if she had to have cancer, she was going to share Jesus with every doctor, nurse, and patient at the University of Virginia (UVA) Cancer Center. So she came prepared with multiple copies of her book *Hope Out Loud Prayers* and handed them out to everyone in the waiting room.

On the way home from her first radiation treatment, Jen said, "Mom, I think God allowed me to have cancer so I can share Jesus with more people. Not many people have brain injuries, but tons of people have cancer. God is expanding my influence!"

I'm ashamed to say I was thinking, *I'm exhausted. Lord, please use another family.*

Have you ever felt like that, as if you couldn't handle one more problem? Maybe you've been drowning in weariness or consumed by darkness. Struggling to understand why a loving God would allow you to endure more pain.

I was feeling sorry for myself, when God revealed something to me. For decades before our car wreck, I was leading Bible studies and prayer groups in my home, at church, and at my kids' Christian school. Yet I hadn't personally led a single person to faith in Christ since I was five years old, when I asked my friend Kim on the swing set if she knew Jesus. I was helping women study God's Word and be better moms and wives, but I was surrounding myself with church ladies. I wasn't reaching out to the hurting and broken. Jesus said, "Healthy people don't need a doctor—sick people do. I have come to call not those who think they are righteous, but those who know they are sinners" (Luke 5:31–32 NLT).

Honestly, I was so busy helping my church friends become healthier, I didn't even notice I was neglecting to share the hope of Jesus with those who were the most broken, wounded, and in need of a savior.

Before our car wreck, I spent most of my evenings at the baseball field, football field, soccer field, or basketball court watching Jen cheer and play soccer or my son, Josh, play every sport imaginable. Often I would encourage other moms on the sidelines. Sometimes I even had the nerve to ask, "How can I pray for you?" But I never had enough boldness to ask, "Do you have a personal relationship with Jesus?" Instead of offending people, I wanted people to like me. Even though I'd been on several mission trips when I was in college, somehow it seemed more difficult to share the gospel at home, where I assumed everyone knew about Jesus.

When was the last time you led a friend to Jesus or invited a neighbor to go to church? Life gets busy. It's easy to get distracted doing lots of great things and miss the most important thing, which is sharing the hope found in Jesus with those around you. Be encouraged. God has a special plan and purpose for you. Your story enables you to relate to the hurts of others, and it gives you an open door to share the love of Jesus. Sharing the real story of how God has met, and is meeting, you in your most tender places proclaims to others that He is real and He is faithful.

WHO IS NORMAL ANYWAY?

When Jen first came home from the hospital, I worked so hard to help her get back to normal. It didn't take me long to figure out that we were no longer destined for normal. I could hardly relate to normal people anymore. I'd go to lunch with friends who would fret over their home renovations, their Target returns, or their plans for their kids' birthday parties. In my pain, their "normal" problems seemed so frivolous. I wanted to scream, "That's not a problem! You don't have problems when you can't decide on a paint color!" Witnessing their normal accentuated my pain. It wasn't their fault; they had no idea their daily concerns reminded me that my daughter would never be the same again.

Have you ever longed for normal? Have you wished you could go back in time to how things were before your family was broken? Before you were broken? Maybe you were born into a family that was already broken or you were born with physical limitations and that was your normal. Many days I couldn't even remember what life before our accident looked or felt like. I wanted to curl up at home in self-pity, but Jen needed to go to therapy sessions and doctors' appointments. One day, almost as if Jen could read my mind, she said, "Well, who is normal anyway?"

About that time, a friend came knocking at the door. I knew she had a child with a disability. I had prayed for her often, but I'd always passed right by her house and never stopped. Maybe because I didn't know what to say. Maybe because I couldn't fully relate to her. Or maybe I assumed she couldn't relate to me. Maybe I was one of those "normal" people who would remind her that her life was anything but normal. Not anymore. Our brokenness knit us together. And sitting on my couch, I got to ask her what I hadn't asked anyone face-to-face since I was five years old: "Do you have a personal relationship with Jesus?" And suddenly I didn't feel broken anymore. I felt useful. I had purpose.

YOUR PAIN HAS AN ETERNAL PURPOSE

I believe God allowed me to be wounded so I would notice hurting people all around me and risk moving beyond the comfort of my church walls and Bible-study friends to share the gospel. My wounds changed my destiny. Yes, life is much harder, but God is using me in far greater ways. My pain has given me a new voice and an urgency to share Jesus. In our physical and emotional brokenness, the one thing that gives me hope is when God uses our family's story to change someone else's story. That's a beauty mark. Every time God allows

our story to touch someone else's story, my wounds are being transformed into purpose. Not just any purpose, but one that is making a
difference for eternity. I needed to know that there was a reason for
our suffering. People are that reason.

The same way my wounds opened my eyes to hurting people,
Jesus's wounds brought Him face-to-face with hurting people, including the two criminals hanging on crosses by His side. Have you ever
wondered why Jesus had to die on a cross? I mean, if He had come into
the world in any other era, His death might have been more humane
or more private, or at least less humiliating. But God, in His sover-
eignty, chose that method of dying in that year on that day, putting
His Son, Jesus, eye to eye with two broken people who needed a savior.

ONE HEART IS CHANGED

In that isolated event, for a moment in time, it may have seemed as
if the Son of God's pain had no purpose. Now, in light of the resurrection, we understand that Jesus was providing a way of salvation for
the world. But for a little while, it could have seemed like the greatest
waste of a life to all of those watching, especially to His followers. It
appeared that His suffering was all in vain. Jesus cried, "Father, forgive
them" over His abusers, and they went right on abusing Him. No
one stopped. No one had a change of heart. Even the criminals dying
beside Him kept hurling insults at Him. Then sometime between His
declaration of forgiveness and His physical death, one heart changed.
One criminal found redemption while Jesus was suffering on the cross.

In the centuries that followed His death, millions of lives would
be changed, including mine. Maybe yours. But in that moment,

while Jesus was still alive on the cross to see it, I have to believe that God in His mercy allowed the redemption of one life to illustrate once and for all that our pain has a purpose. People are the purpose.

Luke 23 describes this powerful interaction:

> Two other men, both criminals, were also led out with [Jesus] to be executed....
>
> One of the criminals who hung there hurled insults at him: "Aren't you the Messiah? Save yourself and us!"
>
> But the other criminal rebuked him. "Don't you fear God," he said, "since you are under the same sentence? We are punished justly, for we are getting what our deeds deserve. But this man has done nothing wrong."
>
> Then he said, "Jesus, remember me when you come into your kingdom."
>
> Jesus answered him, "Truly I tell you, today you will be with me in paradise." (vv. 32, 39–43)

In the middle of Jesus's suffering, when He was most wounded, God the Father allowed His Son to make a difference in the life of another. He gave Jesus's pain purpose. A beauty mark. He allowed His perfect, holy Son to come in contact with and share the same wounds as someone who would normally never be able to relate to Him. He created this divine collision through unspeakable brokenness for one life to heal another life for eternity. Jesus, while He was dying, was intentional about saving others. He modeled for us what it is to care for others in the midst of our own suffering. Jesus's scars were being used to turn something ugly into something beautiful.

IS IT WORTH IT?

So is our suffering worth it? Is God's purpose worth your pain? If you asked me, "Linda, is the pain your daughter faces every day worth saving someone else's life?" I'd really rather you not ask. As Jen and I travel together, speaking to audiences around the country, I know our pain is what allows people to relate to us. I know our pain has helped people we never could have helped before. But if you asked me, "If you had it in your power to reverse what you've endured to spare your daughter this pain, would you?" Yes, I would.

Of course.

Would you protect your children from pain if you could? Most parents would never choose to watch their children suffer. My husband, who was driving our van that day, often says, "I would have missed the drunk driver if I could have, but I never saw him coming."

Jen's life wasn't in my hands. I had no control over what God allowed my family to endure. While the salvation of other people eases my pain, as a mother I never could have chosen the accident. That's the beautiful thing about the cross. Jesus did have a choice. He had the power to stop it. He could have called on the angels to save Him, and they would have spared Him in a second. But He couldn't save Himself *and* us. He chose us.

Even more remarkable to this mother, His Father had the power to stop it. I might be able to choose pain for myself if I knew it had an eternal purpose, but I couldn't choose it for my child. God the

Father left His only Son on the cross because He chose to save you and me instead. He thought we were worth it. That's how much He loves us. It's how much He loves *you*.

DO YOU SEE JESUS?

I sometimes wonder how a person could be hanging right beside Jesus on a cross and miss Him. Both men were criminals. Both men were dying. Both men were eye to eye with Jesus. Their suffering was, in the most explicit way, a divine setup for them to see their Savior. But only one man recognized who was there.

One thief questioned, "Aren't you the Messiah? Save yourself and us" (Luke 23:39). He didn't realize those options were mutually exclusive. If Jesus had saved Himself, He couldn't have saved us.

The other thief understood that his sin was to blame for his problems and saw Jesus as his only hope. "We are punished justly, for we are getting what our deeds deserve," he said. "But this man has done nothing wrong" (v. 41).

Then, turning from his fellow prisoner toward the Christ, he begged, "Jesus, remember me when you come into your kingdom" (v. 42).

This man called on the name of Jesus and asked Jesus to remember him. Jesus answered that He would do much more than remember him. He promised, "Today you will be with me in paradise" (v. 43).

When Jesus is your Savior, you aren't only on His mind; you're in His presence forever. He is your escort, walking beside you, holding your hand. Jen recently wrote in her journal, "Knowing that I don't have to go through one day alone relieves the pressure. Jesus is my companion forever! He gives me the peace of His presence." Her words are a reminder that although bad things still happen in this sinful world, Jesus promises to be with us, right in the middle of our suffering. All we have to do is call on His name.

Christmas 2006 fell a few weeks after Jen had emerged from her coma. She was still mostly lifeless, strapped into a wheelchair because she couldn't sit up on her own. This was before she was speaking to us. My friend Pam and I wheeled her outside to get some fresh air. Jen started one of her episodes of thrashing and moaning, which is common for coma patients as they adjust to their new discomforts. Pam and I started singing "Silent Night" to calm her down, and after a few measures, Jen started singing with us. By the end, her face was glowing and she was smiling and staring to the upper left as if her eyes were fixed on something. Then suddenly she shouted, "Amen!" She was still gazing upward and to the left.

Something about the joy on her face made me ask, "Jen, do you see Jesus?"

"*Yes!* Don't you see Him?" she answered. "He's standing right beside me."

With a smile spread across her face, Jen was beaming. Oh, how I wished I could see what she was seeing. She was completely blind from her brain injury and couldn't even see me, her own mother. Yet God somehow revealed Himself to her. I'm not sure what Jen saw, but I believe Jesus made Himself known in the right place at the right time in exactly the right way so that she would see Him. My constant prayer for Jen was that she would continue to sense the presence of God when she was in pain.

That is also my prayer for you. I don't know how this book ended up in your hands, but I've been praying that in this place, at this time, in some way, you will see Jesus as the answer to your pain. I pray you'll know that He does more than remember your pain or repurpose it; He is *with you* in it. His presence is real. He's near. He whispers to your heart, "You will be with me in paradise."

Like the thief on the cross next to Jesus who acknowledged that he was a sinner and asked Jesus to remember him, all you have to do is ask, "Jesus, remember me and save me." When you do, you can depend on the apostle Paul's reliable assurance: "Everyone who calls on the name of the Lord will be saved" (Rom. 10:13).

EARTHLY FACT VERSUS HEAVENLY REALITY

One of my dearest girlfriends found one of her friends just moments after he had committed suicide. He was a believer in Jesus but still struggled with severe depression. It took my friend months to make sense of why God didn't stop it, and she was plagued with thoughts that her actions or inaction may have contributed to his decision. After months of counseling and reflection, she finally understood that the only way for her to find peace was to separate the earthly facts from the heavenly realities.

> **Earthly fact:** Someone she was close to committed suicide, and she couldn't stop it.
> **Heavenly reality:** He entered into the presence of Jesus, where there is no more sorrow or tears, and one day she will be there too.

This concept—separating earthly facts from heavenly realities—has been incredibly helpful for me. I think it's the same principle we witness in Jesus's statement to the thief on the cross when He began with the word *truly* (earthly fact) and ended with the word *paradise* (heavenly reality).

> **Earthly fact:** *Truly* I tell you, you are going to die a painful death on this cross.
>
> **Heavenly reality:** Today you will be with Me in *paradise*, where there will be no more pain.

Sometimes the only way we can continue to face the facts of our earthly experience is by keeping our focus on the unchangeable heavenly realities. On days when I'm really struggling, I make a list.

Earthly Fact	Heavenly Reality
I feel overwhelmed.	I can do all things through Christ who gives me strength.
Jen will never be normal.	Jen gets to experience the supernatural daily.
Josh's childhood was altered.	Josh's wounds made him passionate about helping others.
Andy has prostate cancer.	God has already ordained every day of Andy's life.
Jen has thyroid cancer.	God's plans for Jen are for His greater glory.
Andy and I have chronic daily nerve pain from our injuries.	We'll have perfect bodies in heaven forever.

When I compare these statements side by side, I realize that the earthly facts are temporary but the heavenly realities last forever.

The apostle Paul explained it this way: "Our light and momentary troubles are achieving for us an eternal glory that far outweighs them all. So we fix our eyes not on what is seen, but on what is unseen, since what is seen [earthly fact] is temporary, but what is unseen [heavenly reality] is eternal" (2 Cor. 4:17–18).

LIFE IS A DOT

One of our family's healthy coping mechanisms for pain is to remind ourselves, "This life is just a dot." That means our short time on this earth is a dot on the timeline of all eternity in heaven with Jesus, where there will be no more pain or suffering. In fact, for a season I said that phrase so many times each day that Jen started to call me "Polka Dot"! We can survive our temporary earthly experience one day at a time with God's help when we know our heavenly reality is endless.

Now walk with me one step further. What if your temporary earthly fact could change someone else's heavenly reality forever? For example, what if God used the fact that you lost someone you loved to ensure that others you love aren't lost forever? What if God used the fact that you were abused to rescue someone else from abuse? I'm not asking you if it would be worth it or which you would choose. Often we don't get to choose what happens to us. Sometimes we can't change our earthly facts. But forgiveness frees us from thinking about whether we would choose them, who is to blame, or who should have stopped it. And when we use our earthly facts to change someone else's heavenly reality, our wounds are transformed into beauty marks.

ANNIE'S STORY

My friend Lauren's precious baby, Annie, went to heaven after living only three hours. There are no words to describe Lauren's pain and heartache. We had the privilege of being with Lauren on the day she visited the funeral home and picked up a beautiful silver double-heart necklace with Annie's fingerprint and footprint on it. As I clasped the necklace for Lauren, she announced through her tears that every time someone asked her about it, she would share the love of Jesus. That way, Annie's short-lived, precious life would have eternal purpose every day.

Lauren's earthly reality was that she lost her baby. No one could change that. Her heavenly reality was that Annie had been freed from the pain and suffering of this world. She was spending her life in the arms of Jesus. Lauren's pain was transformed into a beauty mark. Her wound gave her eternal purpose when she used Annie's story to share the love and faithfulness of Jesus with others. Some days that lessens Lauren's pain.

Perhaps you've suffered a devastating loss. God knows how hard it is. May you hear Him whisper to your heart today, "I have made you and I will carry you; I will sustain you and I will rescue you" (Isa. 46:4).

FIX ME VERSUS USE ME

Our flesh tends to focus on our pain instead of our purpose. Like the first thief on the cross, we cry, "Save us. Fix us. Stop this!" In the years since the accident, I've noticed that instead of asking God to fix her, Jen asks Him to use her.

One night, a few months after Jen was released from the hospital, Andy, Josh, and I were kneeling around her bed praying over her and begging God to heal her. Andy was rubbing Jen's feet because she was in so much pain and he wanted to calm her so she could go to sleep. We were asking God to fix Jen's eyes, fix her memory, fix her headaches. We prayed healing every night over every part of her body and soul. There's nothing wrong with that. Any loving parent would do that.

Then right in the middle of our prayer, Jen started praying. It was one of those times she was so full of the Spirit and seemed to be right in God's presence.

She said, "Lord, did I meet all of Your expectations today? Did I fulfill all the plans You had for me to do today?"

Once again, I was totally blown away.

I thought, *How could God have expectations of a teenager with a brain injury? Certainly He understands our earthly reality right now, and He can put the heavenly stuff on hold.*

That wasn't how Jen thought. She only wanted to know if she had met all of God's expectations for her. She wanted God to use her for His glory to make a difference in the lives of others. Hearing Jen pray created a shift in me. I stopped begging, "God, fix me," and started praying, "God, use me."

When I review the ten years since our accident, the biggest transformation in me and my family is that we're now sharing the gospel everywhere we go. We've seen thousands of people pray to receive Jesus as their personal Lord and Savior. God has opened doors of opportunity through our tragedy. Everywhere we go to speak, the first question we ask is, "Can we talk about Jesus?"

Plus, since Jen's brain injury frees her to be totally uninhibited, she doesn't care what anyone thinks about her. She shares Jesus on airplanes, at the grocery store, at the YMCA—basically everywhere she goes! Jen simply smiles and says, "Do you know Jesus? He wants to be with you in heaven forever!" Then Andy and I start sharing the gospel because we're with Jen. She'll ask the awkward question to start the conversation and leave the rest to us. It's almost as if God rewired my daughter to automatically ask the question I wasn't sure how to broach for thirty-five years.

Jen's brain injury has made her voice louder and stronger. Her pain gives her credibility, and people have never told her they don't want to hear what she has to say.

Jen often reminds me, "Mom, we have the secret, the answer to life. We need to share it with everyone we meet because our time is short."

Even strangers admire Jen for the wounds she has endured, and they usually can't comprehend her joy in the midst of suffering. It can only be explained as the presence of Christ in her. She says, "I don't want to be remembered as the girl with the brain injury but as the girl who loved Jesus with all of her heart!"

Do you remember the story at the beginning of this chapter when Jen handed out copies of her prayer book at the cancer center? Well, last year our family had the privilege of speaking on a Sunday morning at a church in Charlottesville, just minutes away from the UVA Cancer Center. A beautiful, precious lady with no hair, wearing a blue knit hat, came up to Jen after the service. She was holding a copy of Jen's book *Hope Out Loud Prayers* that looked beaten up and torn.

She gushed, "When I heard you were speaking, Jen, I couldn't wait to come meet you. You see, one of the nurses at the cancer center saved your prayer book and gave it to me. I've been praying your prayers and quoting Scripture for two years, and I even accepted Jesus! Now I'm cancer free! I'm a cancer survivor!"

My heart was overflowing with joy. Could she have been the reason God allowed Jen to have cancer? If so, that was an eternal purpose. A few months later, we learned that our new friend had passed away. At first, my heart was so sad. We thought her cancer was healed. But Jen quickly reminded me, "Mom, she is healed. She is in heaven!"

> **Earthly fact:** My daughter had cancer.
> **Heavenly reality:** This friend will be with us in heaven forever because Jen had cancer at the right time. Another beauty mark.

By contrasting earthly facts with heavenly realities, I never mean to minimize the suffering we face. When our earthly facts are too overwhelming for us to bear, God never abandons us. In fact, He may be closer than ever.

Chapter 5

WHO SHOULD HOLD YOUR RAINBOW TURKEY?

Leave it all in the Hands that were wounded for you.

Elisabeth Elliot, *Keep a Quiet Heart*

My son, Josh, was a cute, full-throttle preschooler. He had curly blond hair, blue eyes, and a big, wide smile. Josh was the kid who sang the loudest in the holiday programs, played the hardest on the playground, and always bear-hugged his teacher. Some days I wish I could turn back time to preschool, when all of life's biggest problems could still be solved with a lollipop!

I loved picking Josh up from preschool. I'd park my car and walk inside the little brick church to his classroom, which exploded with primary colors and oversize artwork. The students' latest handcrafted masterpieces lined the hallway leading up to the classroom door. As soon as he saw me, Josh's face would light up as if we'd been separated for years. After a quick hug, he'd run into the hall to find the picture with his name written in inverted or slanted letters, frantically telling me why his artwork was so special and making me promise to save it forever. The week before Thanksgiving, he thrust a rainbow-colored paper turkey toward me that he'd made by tracing his little hand.

"Mom, hold this!" he insisted, shoving his treasured artwork into my hands and running outside to play with the other boys.

After wild chasing and riotous wrestling, he came back sweaty and dirty to the group of chattering moms and asked, "Mom, where's my turkey?"

If you've ever been the mother of an energetic preschool boy, you know exactly what I'm talking about. They race through life collecting bumps and bruises, not caring if their clothes get ruined or their skin gets scraped. But they have full confidence that whatever they place in your hands will be safe and secure when they return. It's a beautiful, reckless trust that whatever is given to Mama will survive all threats of disaster.

They do the same thing with broken treasures.

"Mom, fix this!"

I can't tell you how many broken parts and pieces were placed in my hands during those precious years, with the full expectation that I could resurrect superheroes, revive remote-control cars, and reconstruct Lego buildings. It was a bold and certain hope that matched his big, audacious messes.

MY FATHER'S HANDS

God longs for us to have that same childlike faith in Him, trusting that whatever we place in His hands is completely safe and secure. We may be broken, wounded, and falling to pieces, but when we trust those pieces to Him, He can and will sustain us through our darkest days.

Handling the messy stuff of daily living is what a shepherd does. Jesus is the good shepherd, and we are His sheep. He guides and protects us one day, one step at a time. Jesus assures us, "My sheep listen to my voice; I know them, and they follow me. I give them eternal life, and they shall never perish; no one will snatch them out of my hand. My Father, who has given them to me, is greater than all; no one can snatch them out of my Father's hand" (John 10:27–29). His hands are a safe place.

When I'm crumbling, when I start to spiral downward, when it hurts too much to hope, I secure my spirit where I know it will be safe: my Father's hands. On my most difficult days, I curl up in the oversize chair in my living room and imagine that God is cradling me in His strong, giant hands. Sometimes I can't do anything other than cry. I can't even form the words to pray, but I sit there and visualize His hands surrounding me until my spirit starts to grow stronger.

I bet you've had those kinds of days. Maybe today you need to know you're safe and secure in your Father's hands. If you're anxious or afraid, you can rest in God's everlasting arms. You can share the deepest desires and longings of your heart with Him as He holds you tightly. Choose your favorite chair and rest in His love.

FULL ACCESS

When Jesus was hanging on the cross, the sky got dark and the curtain of the temple was torn in two. "Jesus called out with a loud voice, 'Father, into your hands I commit my spirit.' When he had said this, he breathed his last" (Luke 23:46).

Have you ever felt as if the sun has stopped shining on you? For the last three hours of Jesus's life, the sun stopped shining on Him as the sin of the world rested on His shoulders. Then it was finished. Salvation was complete. The veil in the temple tore in half as a symbol that you and I could now come close to God. The curtain that separated God's holy dwelling from the place where the common, sinful people waited would never again stop us from coming closer. Jesus was temporarily forsaken by His Father so that we could gain full access to Him.

But Jesus also gave us another gift. Before He died, He used His last ounce of strength to proclaim another healing prescription in a loud voice for everyone nearby to hear. He quoted the words Jewish fathers taught their children to pray before they went to bed at night and the lights went out until morning: "Into your hands I commit my spirit" (Ps. 31:5). Only this time, Jesus added the word *Father*. "Father, into your hands I commit my spirit" (Luke 23:46).

At the very moment He was dying to give us the right to become the children of God, Jesus taught us to pray the traditional children's bedtime prayer from Psalm 31, but with a twist.[4] He gave us permission to add the word *Father*.

HEALING BEGINS WITH A PERSONAL RELATIONSHIP

Of all the words Jesus spoke on the cross, these are the most healing for me. They remind me that my healing doesn't depend on me or my ability to forgive or find purpose for my scars. My healing begins with a personal relationship with my Father.

When I don't know what to do or where to turn, I run to my Father. When I'm overwhelmed with the uncertainty of Jen's future or feel as though I've reached the end of my strength, I take a deep breath and say what Jesus said: "Father, into your hands I commit my spirit." I can't describe the relief that washes over me when I know my Father is holding my fragile spirit securely in His strong and loving hands. I can start to breathe again. I can start to think again. I can put one foot in front of the other and keep moving. Healing happens when I don't have to put any effort into holding myself together. I place that job in my Father's hands.

Maybe you're thinking, *I want to be healed, but I feel so unworthy.* You may hear about wholeness and love, but you can't even begin to comprehend it because you have no memory of healthy love. Jesus longs to have a personal relationship with you. He wants to be your companion, the one you run to and with whom you share everything. You can trust Him. There is nothing you can say or do to make Him stop loving you. He will never leave you or abandon you.

GOD HOLDS OUR WOUNDS TOGETHER

Just as a physical wound has to be bandaged again to heal once it is cleaned out and medicated with an antibiotic, the same is true of our emotional wounds. After we open our emotional wounds, extending forgiveness and seeking eternal purpose in our pain, we can wrap them up with clean bandages and return them to the hands of our heavenly Father, saying, *"Father, into Your hands I commit my spirit."*

Each one of us has a spirit at the very core of our being. The Greek word used in Luke's gospel is *pneuma*. It's a God awareness that animates the body and the soul. Jesus was built the same way. When He committed His spirit into God's hands, He was saying, in essence, "Father, I place the very essence of who I am, the part of Me that lives on forever, the part of Me that gives hope and purpose to the rest of Me, into Your hands."

Your spirit is essential to your thriving. If your spirit is damaged, the rest of you is damaged. But if your spirit is secure, the rest of you can be dying or falling apart but you'll still have hope. The part of you that matters most will live on with God.

Several years ago, my earthly father had open-heart surgery. I'm still amazed that one day doctors stopped his heart and rewired his arteries and the next day he was eating breakfast and walking down the hall. He was on the path to healing when a staph infection aggressively attacked his body. Because he was too weak to fight it on his own, the doctors had to reopen his chest wound to clean out the infection. The result was one hundred days in intensive care with a gaping chasm in his chest.

I remember looking at the divide in his chest and thinking there was no way it would ever heal on its own. It wouldn't. The wound-care specialists wrapped his chest with a wide, stretchy bandage that held two parts of his flesh together for weeks until it had time to grow back together. Every day they would unwrap the bandage to clean the wound and then quickly rewrap it, securing the wound in a closed position until new flesh could form.

That bandage reminded me of our heavenly Father's hands. Psalm 147:3 assures us, "He heals the brokenhearted and binds up their wounds." He holds our gaping wounds together like a strong and secure bandage so we can apply some of the healing practices we've been learning. Without His care for our most tender places, healing would never be possible.

RELAPSE

A few months ago, I attended a wedding to celebrate a special young couple. I was expecting to enjoy a happy, joyous occasion. I wasn't expecting to run into another guest who had been dishonest and stolen lots of money from our family. The sight of this person ripped open a wound I thought was nearly healed. Bitterness and anger came gushing out. I wanted to leave, but that wouldn't have been kind to the friends who were getting married. This sudden stab of pain caught me off guard. So I took a deep breath and said what Jesus said: "Father, into your hands I commit my spirit."

Guess what? The Father came through for me. He held me together until I could get some perspective on this pain. My joy wasn't stripped from me. Once my spirit was secure, I felt peace. Although I never could have taken the high road on my own, I found the strength to handle myself with grace and dignity.

When Jesus quoted Psalm 31 on the cross—"Into your hands I commit my spirit"—it's almost as though He left a clue for us to go discover a poem that David wrote. Throughout my healing journey, it's been a treasure to me. The psalm is not only about committing our spirits to God through the physical act of dying. It's also about being *trapped.*

> Keep me free from the trap that is set for me,
>   for you are my refuge.
> Into your hands I commit my spirit;
>   deliver me, LORD, my faithful God. (vv. 4–5)

Jesus was about to be trapped in a grave. Talk about the lights going out! He would be buried in darkness and would have to depend completely on His Father to resurrect Him again.

What if Satan's strategy is to cause us to relapse as we're starting to make progress on our healing journeys? He'll do anything to resurrect feelings of rejection, abandonment, neglect, betrayal, failure, loss, or inadequacy. Satan, the enemy of our souls, loves to rip off the scab and make our wounds bleed again. A certain person or place might rub salt into an old wound. Or the Enemy plants a trap that uniquely baits our wounded hearts. Sometimes it can feel more crippling than the original wound. It leaves us doubting whether progress is ever really possible.

SATAN'S NUMBER-ONE GOAL

Satan aggravates wounds from the past to devastate your future.

My friend, please stop and notice those words. Underline them. Highlight them. Write them on a sticky note and post it on your bathroom mirror. Because Satan is deceitful and manipulative, he evokes the painful memories and mistakes of your past. To keep you paralyzed, he twists the dagger that is already in your heart from those old wounds. He is evil, and he wants you to miss the amazing plan God has for your future. You're a threat to Satan. He knows that God can transform your pain into beauty marks and use you in greater ways for His glory.

It's important for you to understand that preventing infection in your wounds requires continuous attention. Often those near you have no intention of hurting you. Satan is the real enemy. He'll twist what people say or do to cause you to take offense. Friend, the only thing you need to take personally is Jesus's offer to place that offense in His Father's hands. The moment your wound rips open, you're vulnerable again. If you don't have a plan for that moment, your default may be an unhealthy form of self-preservation. Make a plan. Your action plan could be to say the words of Jesus aloud: "Father, into your hands I commit my spirit." In other words, "Father, I wrap up my wound and give it to You to hold."

SHEILA'S STORY

After sharing in the birth and nurture of their three children, ages four, six, and seven, Sheila's husband left her for another woman. Sheila had joint custody, which meant that she had to regularly communicate with her ex and the woman who had lured her husband away. Every other weekend, when they exchanged children, Sheila's raw wounds were exposed. She was torturing herself with thoughts of inadequacy and bitterness. Her husband had moved on, but she tormented herself by replaying scenes of what she could have or should have done differently. The constant rewounding was draining the life out of her.

If you can relate to Sheila, my heart is aching for you right now. I can't begin to imagine the emotional pain and trauma you experience daily. I'm asking God to fill you with His immeasurable strength and courage for the journey. I know He is with you and sees every tear. The psalmist wrote, "You keep track of all my sorrows. You have collected all my tears in your bottle. You have recorded each one in your book" (Ps. 56:8 NLT).

One weekend when Sheila didn't have her kids, a girlfriend invited her to enjoy a few drinks and meet some new people. What started out as a simple diversion led to an alcohol addiction that quickly spiraled out of control.

"When you drink," Sheila shared with me, "all the pressure and anxiety disappears. You don't have to face the pain. I wasn't happy living as a victim to alcohol addiction, but to stop would make me wide open again to being wounded. To be honest, I was afraid to recover. I was afraid to be vulnerable again to being hurt. Alcohol was my form of self-protection."

When I met Sheila, she had been sober for eighteen months, one week, and three days. Through her local church and Alcoholics Anonymous groups, she had found the support to choose God as her protector rather than trusting herself for protection. Rather than continuing to rehearse her record of sorrows, she released them to the One who held her tears.

Though I don't pretend to believe that breaking addiction is simple or easy, shifting your energies from self-preservation to trusting your Creator makes it possible. You may need to meet with a counselor to work through the root of your pain. You need a community of accountability. But in those moments when the scab is unexpectedly torn away and your wound starts bleeding again, your Maker can provide the emergency triage you need. In that moment you have to decide whom you'll trust—yourself or your Savior.

ADDICTIVE BEHAVIORS

Unhealed wounds can trigger a relapse into addictive behaviors. Since most addicts grew up in families that wounded them, many experience "deep sadness, feelings of shame, and loneliness."[5] I've interviewed hundreds of women fighting addictions, many of whom revealed that they were afraid of failure and feeling pain again. It was shocking to discover how many women were believing the lie that a substance or addictive habit was making their lives more bearable. In reality, it was controlling them and causing both them and their loved ones to suffer.

Dear friend, I don't know the details and nuances of your pain. But I do know your Enemy. He has a counterfeit plan for your life. He wins when we torture ourselves by overindulging, neglecting our needs, comparing ourselves with others, dwelling on painful memories, or imagining future painful scenarios. All of these end in "self" and keep us from the One who came to give us abundant life (see John 10:10).

Though life can be painful, you don't have to keep hurting. When you relapse into destructive thoughts or behaviors, secure your spirit. Instead of repeating the offense over and over in your head—what he said or what she meant or what you should have said—try saying what Jesus said: "Father, into your hands I commit my spirit."

Every time I speak those words, an unexplainable peace washes over me. It takes the burden and pressure off me and puts them in God's sovereign hands.

When your heart starts throbbing in pain again, you can gently wrap up your wound by securing your spirit and placing it in God's hands to hold.

Jen recently started saying these words during her bedtime prayers. Before she closes her eyes, she prays aloud, "Father, into Your hands I commit my spirit." In other words, she's saying, "Father, hold me in Your everlasting arms and keep me safe and secure while

I sleep. Hold my wounds and fill my mind with Your peace." Try praying that tonight as your head touches the pillow.

TWO STORIES

Two biblical stories, one from 2 Chronicles 24 in the Old Testament and one from Acts 7 in the New, are strikingly similar but have remarkably different outcomes. I'm going to share the arc of each and let you discover the meaning for yourself. I encourage you to read these stories in their entirety.

The first story is about a guy named Zechariah, who was full of God's Spirit (2 Chron. 24:20). King Joash ordered that Zechariah be stoned to death (v. 21), and as he was dying, Zechariah asked God for vengeance: "May the LORD see this and call you [Joash] to account" (v. 22). Soon after, Joash was severely wounded in battle and then assassinated in his bed and forgotten in a commoner's tomb (vv. 23–25).

The second story is about a guy named Stephen, who was full of God's Spirit (Acts 7:55). Religious leaders ordered that Stephen be stoned to death, and Saul held the coats of those who did it (v. 58). As he was dying, Stephen asked God to pardon his executioners. He prayed what Jesus prayed on the cross: "Lord Jesus, receive my spirit…. Lord, do not hold this sin against them" (vv. 59–60). Soon after, Saul experienced a radical transformation (9:1–31) and became the first person to take the good news of salvation to Europe. His message of hope eventually spread throughout the world. In fact, the New Testament describes much of his story.

I'd like to leave you with some final questions as you weigh these two accounts: What good did vengeance accomplish for Zechariah? Did it undo his wounds?

You may understand Zechariah's prayer if you've been tempted to repay evil with evil. If you exacted revenge, did it take away your pain or make you feel worse? Many who get vengeance report that it didn't relieve the pain as they imagined it would.

If you're reading this book, you've most likely benefited from the spread of Christianity that began with a guy named Saul, who is better known as Paul. What if *he* was changed because Stephen, his victim, chose to ask God not for vengeance but for forgiveness?

As he was dying, Stephen, the first Christian martyr, prayed essentially the same prayer Jesus said on the cross: "Lord Jesus, receive my spirit" (Acts 7:59). His pain was transformed into a beauty mark of purpose, and I believe that your pain is also being redeemed.

Toward that end, there's something else you can practice every day to mend your wounded heart and change your destiny.

Chapter 6

A CAUTIONARY TALE OF TWO GRANDMOTHERS

It is one of the most beautiful compensations of life that no man can sincerely try to help another without helping himself.

Ralph Waldo Emerson

Both of my grandmothers outlived their husbands. One grandfather died of a heart attack a few years after retiring. The other died of lung cancer at age eighty-six. As was common in their generation, neither grandmother had spent much time driving a car or balancing a checkbook. In addition to the grief of losing their best friends, the thought of living alone after decades of marriage was daunting.

If you've lost a husband to death, disease, infidelity, or abandonment, please allow God to hold you right now and speak to your heart that you are never alone. If you've never been married, God's gentle whisper is the same: He promises to be your husband and to never leave you or forsake you. "For your Maker is your husband—the LORD Almighty is his name" (Isa. 54:5). God will be your protector, your provider, and your best friend.

My Grammy Helen was a beautiful, vivacious woman. She had a tendency to be domineering at times, but we laughed about it and loved her all the same. Sadly, after her husband died, she pulled the drapes shut and became a recluse in her home. She stopped attending social functions and church. Neighbors tried to help her, but she often rejected their help. My family tried to move her to the town where we lived, but she refused.

She finally agreed to come stay with us for a while and participate in my sister's wedding plans, but she never got on the plane. She wouldn't make the trip. She eventually died isolated and alone. It broke my heart because I loved her dearly but I couldn't "fix" her. When I was a little girl, every afternoon Grammy Helen and I would talk for hours and sip hot tea with a teaspoonful of cream and sugar. I would often sleep with her, and we would tell secrets. Of course, I thought it was perfectly normal that my grandpa had his own bedroom across the hallway. I have many precious memories of her.

Grammy Helen had so much potential to help others. She could have allowed God to transform her pain into purpose, but instead, she chose to focus on her own hurts and missed God's best for her later years.

A LEGACY OF SERVING

My other grandmother, equally devastated when she lost her spouse, continued to do what she had done well for years, laughing and serving others. Grammy Jean was the kind of woman who would host all the church parties but would also leave a mannequin on the toilet so you'd open the bathroom door and think you'd walked in on somebody! She had been serving in the same church for half a century when she lost her husband.

Instead of backing out of her duties, she took on more. She lived next to the church, where she could see everything that happened on the property. Every time there were cars in the parking lot, she would walk over to see if anybody needed help. One time she even showed up for a men's prayer meeting! She knitted baby blankets for every new mom, helped with childcare, cooked meals for other widows, and constantly entertained guests in her home. Jean Currie was a tireless servant until age ninety.

In case you think your story is too painful to be beautiful, you need to know something else about Grammy Jean. The truly amazing thing about her life wasn't only her service; it was also the scars and wounds she overcame. Her mother died of pneumonia when she was just three years old, leaving her father with two little girls and an infant to raise. In desperation, he hastily married the children's nurse. It wasn't long before she physically and emotionally abused my grandmother so severely that Grammy Jean's own father helped her run away from home when she was twelve years old. Grammy Jean grew up without the love of a mother, yet she became one of the greatest wives and mothers I have ever known.

If your life isn't how you pictured it would be, don't give up. Grammy Jean's story is proof that no wound is so great that God can't redeem it and use it to bless others.

In her ninetieth year, we finally moved Grammy Jean into a nursing home in our hometown. My mother, my cousin Heidi, and I were blessed to share her last two years with her. Every time I saw her, she was laughing and singing. I'll never forget walking into her room and seeing her flip through well-worn, wrinkled note cards with Bible verses handwritten on them. She was still memorizing Scripture at ninety-two! Not a visit went by without her telling someone about Jesus or singing about Him. Some of the very last words on her lips were the lyrics of a hymn: "Jesus is the sweetest name I know."[6] My cousin Heidi sang it with her, and then a few days later, Grammy Jean slipped into heaven with a smile on her face.

Both grandmothers suffered from the same soul wound of losing their husbands. The difference was that one served herself and one served others, leaving a beautiful mark on this world and a legacy of faith for her family. Grammy Jean taught us how to serve others and have unwavering faith in God.

On days when I start to slip into the pit of self-pity, their two divergent stories are powerful reminders to me that life and death hang in the balance of how I choose to nurture my wounds. The same is true for you. I'm praying that you will allow God to transform your wounds into beauty marks of purpose. I believe you will be like my grandmother who made a difference until her last breath.

We can choose life together!

WOMAN, YOUR SON

Jesus knew firsthand the restorative power of serving. He "did not come to be served, but to serve, and to give his life … for many" (Matt. 20:28). The prospect of helping others was His whole motivation for leaving heaven.

Even while He was suffering on the cross, He was serving others. He publicly forgave the soldiers who were driving the spikes into His hands. He promised the thief dying next to Him eternal life moments after he taunted Jesus. And my personal favorite: Jesus even made provision for His mother's future while His own life was coming to an end.

My secret confession is that I'm a complete sucker for the mother-and-son bond. It's not even a secret. Everyone close to me knows that I'll stay up until two o'clock in the morning or drive five hours to a baseball game if I think I might get even thirty seconds face-to-face with my adult son. And when he initiates spending time with me or does anything that remotely resembles taking care of me, it's all over. He's captured my heart, a reloaded credit card, and anything else he wants on a silver platter!

As the conspicuously proud mother of a son, I think the words Jesus directed to His mother on the cross are some of the most precious in all of Scripture:

> Near the cross of Jesus stood his mother, his mother's sister, Mary the wife of Clopas, and Mary Magdalene. When Jesus saw his mother there, and the disciple whom he loved standing nearby, he said to her, "Woman, here is your son," and to the disciple, "Here is your mother." From that time on, this disciple took her into his home. (John 19:25–27)

In the midst of His pain, Jesus noticed His mother standing "near the cross." Jesus didn't call her "Mother," perhaps to protect her privacy or protect her from harm. After all, she was a private woman who kept her feelings close to her heart (see Luke 2:19). He would have known that. The New Living Translation (NLT) uses the words "dear woman," which show respect and endearment. Part of the message here is that you can stay near Jesus when you're hurting because you are near and dear to His heart.

The other part of the message is that while Jesus was wounded, He was helping and serving others. Jesus was showing compassion and caring for His mother instead of focusing on Himself.

Don't you think Jesus was leaving us a powerful remedy for our pain? When you're suffering, look to the needs of others. Whom can you help? Whom can you serve?

Think about it. This is the one statement Jesus spoke on the cross that He really didn't have to say publicly. First of all, this statement didn't fulfill any prophecies as some of the others did. It wasn't a quote from Psalms or a prediction of Isaiah or even a prayer. It was a Jesus original from the cross. Second, He could easily have pulled John the disciple aside at the Last Supper the night before and said, "Hey, dude, I need you to take care of My mom after I'm gone." It's not as if He didn't know from the beginning of time that this moment was coming. Or He could have waited until He came back to life to finish up His family business. He had plenty of opportunities after His resurrection when He appeared to His disciples and other witnesses to make arrangements for Mary's future.

Instead, Jesus chose the moment when He was most wounded to model servanthood. He modeled what I've discovered to be true in my own experience: sometimes the only way to survive or make sense of your own pain is to help someone else.

HELPING IS HEALING

It didn't take long for our family to notice that one of the only times Jen felt relief from her suffering was when she was helping others. The more her brain started to heal, the more she started to hurt everywhere. Her body was hypersensitive. It hurt when anyone touched her. She screamed in the shower because the water felt like thousands of needles penetrating her body. It was almost as though her brain would fixate on the pain and intensify her agony. Every time she ate, her body could feel the digestion process so intensely that she would double over with stomach cramps. For at least five years, Jen had severe headaches. The pain made it very hard for her to function around people or noise. However, if she saw a lady in a wheelchair or a child who was crying, she would immediately forget she was hurting.

She would say, "How can I help you? Can I pray with you?"

All her focus would be on helping instead of hurting. I've seen Jen do this hundreds of times. She might be crying in pain because she walked into a wall she didn't see, but then five minutes later, she can be full of joy if she sees someone who needs her help. When Jen is helping others, it gives her a purpose. Her suffering is transformed into a beauty mark. She is consumed with thoughts of other people instead of her own pain.

When you're aware of one feeling, others fade out of your awareness. So if you're feeling sympathy or compassion for someone else, even for a brief moment, you aren't feeling pain. It doesn't mean the pain goes away, but your focus shifts momentarily away from yourself to someone else.

This is how we began sharing our story and helping others. It was the only way to get a break from our misery. When Jen would walk into a room to help others, she would talk more clearly and function better. Sometimes she would be in horrible pain up until the moment we walked out onstage. I would be thinking, *This is a terrible idea. We should never have come.* Then the moment she started talking, her whole countenance would be transformed.

Recently I captured a few photos of Jen helping other girls, and I had to blink my eyes and do a double take because I was shocked to catch a glimpse of her looking like she did before her accident. It stopped my heart. The typical droop on one side of her face that is common with brain-injury survivors intermittently disappears while she is helping others. I have no idea whether there is even a medical explanation for this. I only know that when she's serving, she looks different and acts differently. In those moments Jen reflects Jesus more than ever.

Similarly, when Jen prays for others, that's the only time I don't have to give her any cues to help her memory. Because of Jen's memory problems, she can't plan in advance what she's going to pray. She's an instrument God speaks through. She often giggles with excitement during her prayers as God brings verses and Bible stories to mind. I'm often shocked at the names and details she can remember, especially since she might not remember what day of the week it is or what she ate for breakfast! It's as if she's healing right before my eyes when she's serving others.

As you can imagine, we've scheduled serving into our daily routine for this very reason. A few mornings a week, we lead prayer groups. Other mornings my mom takes Jen to visit people in nursing homes and hospitals. On weekends we travel to speak at events and churches. Some days I think we can't possibly keep up this schedule. Then I think of Jesus on the cross taking care of His mother, and I'm reminded of this truth: if you're helping, you're healing.

SCIENTIFIC EVIDENCE

Bioethics professor Stephen Post has done some fascinating research on altruism and healing. In it he explores the theory of helper therapy, which suggests that helping others is essential to helping yourself. The scientific evidence proving that serving is directly proportional to healing is mind blowing. Here are some of the findings:[7]

- Alcoholics who help other alcoholics in a recovery program are almost twice as likely to avoid alcohol in the first year after treatment compared with those unengaged in helping others. The chances of successfully avoiding alcohol increase from 22 percent to 40 percent when you help others.

- A Stanford University study demonstrated that women with advanced metastatic breast cancer survived twice as long when they were involved in a peer support group where they demonstrated compassion for one another. The women who helped others lived an average of eighteen months, compared with an average of nine months for those not engaged in compassion and emotional support.

- For thirty years, researchers from Cornell University followed 427 wives and mothers from upstate New York. At the end of the study, they concluded that "regardless of number of children, marital status, occupation, education, or social class, those women who engaged in volunteer work to help other people at least once a week lived longer and had better physical functioning." And another study found that seniors who spent at least one hundred hours volunteering each year had about 30 percent fewer physical limitations.

As my girlfriend used to say, science always agrees with Jesus. What are we waiting for? Let's get serving!

STARTING REHAB

When you're in pain and find someone to serve—as Jesus did on the cross when He said to His mother, "Woman, here is your son," and to His disciple, "Here is your mother"—you are actually starting rehab. You are exercising your physical and emotional muscles instead of sitting on the couch, isolated and alone. Have you ever been to rehab for a broken bone or a torn ligament? At first it's painful, but when you consistently do the exercises, stretches, and weight lifting, your wounds begin to heal.

Think of serving as rehab for your wounded heart. The more you serve others, the less pain you'll feel, and your heart will begin to heal over time.

Five months after our car wreck, I had a surgery on my left hand. I already had a steel rod in my left arm, but because of nerve damage, I couldn't lift my wrist or use my left hand. It hung limp. I couldn't even feed Jen through her feeding tube because that required two hands. So the surgeon decided to attempt three tendon transfers on my left hand and wrist. After surgery, my hand and fingers stuck straight out. Stiff as a board. I couldn't move them at all. So if I was going to have any functionality in my hand, I had to go to rehab three times a week.

Rehab was extremely painful. I could hardly bear it at first. I had to retrain my brain. The tendon that turned my wrist over from side to side was now attached to a different place that would raise my wrist. The surgeon never thought I would be able to make a fist again. But guess what? After six months of rehab, countless hours of at-home therapy exercises, and lots of prayer, I did it. I made a fist!

It's still a struggle to use my left hand. My middle finger, ring finger, and pinkie all move together, so I'm only able to type with my left pointer finger. But it hasn't slowed me down. Yes, I have nerve pain in my left hand every day. Yes, it's worse when I'm typing the pages of this book. Is it worth it? A thousand times yes! Why? Because I'm praying with every word I type that God will use my pain to help you heal in ways you never dreamed possible.

JEANETTE AND TONY'S STORY

Every decision Jeanette was being forced to make was a painful reminder of her future. She was helping care for her father-in-law, who was losing his ability to eat and breathe on his own after years of being confined to a wheelchair, when her husband, in his early forties, was diagnosed with the same genetic type of multiple sclerosis (MS). She had to help make decisions about the last few months of her father-in-law's life while watching her husband rapidly lose muscle function, including the ability to pick up their kids in his arms. One of their most painful moments came when she and Tony had to break the news to their son and daughter that they needed to sell their childhood home with a pool and play area because their father could no longer take care of it.

About that time, someone at church invited them to participate in a weekly service opportunity cooking meals and delivering them to homeless people living on the streets less than ten miles from their beloved home. In the midst of losing their home, Jeanette and Tony started serving people who had no homes. "Changing our focus from self to selfless was a game changer for us," Jeanette explains. "It helped keep us out of depression to get out and serve people less fortunate than we were." They discovered rehab for the soul.

The truth is that Tony's uncertain future has motivated him to be more intentional with his children than the average father. He can't pick up his kids, so he picks up Styrofoam to-go boxes and serves food to the homeless, hand in hand with his kids, every Monday night. That's a beauty mark!

PAIN BECOMES PURPOSE

Please don't convince yourself that your story is too painful to ever be beautiful. That's not true. Out of ashes comes beauty. Your pain is never wasted. It gives you a voice and a purpose. It causes you to notice people you wouldn't normally notice. It helps you relate to people with whom you would otherwise have nothing in common. Almost every disability ministry our family has seen was started by someone who has a disabled child or has been touched by disability in some way. Every December we participate in a Christmas toy run started by a family who lost their child one Christmas. I look at my own monthly calendar and realize it's full of opportunities we never would have been afforded if we hadn't been wounded.

What needs do you see around you? What pain and injustice does God reveal to you that others miss? What is one thing you could do today to make a difference in the life of one person? Maybe a simple hug or an "I love you." Cleaning a house while someone is in the hospital. Cooking a meal. Giving someone a gasoline or grocery gift card. Rubbing someone's hands or feet with lotion as that person is lying sick in bed. The possibilities are endless! I get so excited thinking about it. Ask God to open your eyes and put a passion in your heart. Take a moment to be still and write down the things He brings to your mind. You could make a serving list.

Jen and I make a serving list every week. It gives Jen purpose, a reason to get out of bed. Instead of "Who will help me?" Jen says, "Who can I help?" She likes to have someone to serve every day, even if it's as simple as making a handmade card and writing a prayer to give someone hope. Jen also has a prayer wall filled with hundreds of pictures of children and adults she prays for every day. Some of the people pictured on that wall have been healed of cancer and brain tumors; others have chronic pain or disabilities. One boy was in a wheelchair, and now he's walking. At least twenty of the people pictured were once spiritually dead and have come to life in Jesus. We've seen God do the impossible. He delights in doing miracles. Prayer is another way to serve others.

All of us discover needs and gain credibility with those in need because of our own wounds. Pain not only gives us compassion, but it also expands our influence. You and the world have more to gain from your painful days than your easy days. There are three primary ways your wounds will give you new purpose and passion to help others.

1. Mending. You'll get to know God through your healing process in a way you never would have known Him without your wounds. God can redeem whatever has happened in your life and use it for His glory. The apostle Paul declared, "We know that God causes everything to work together for the good of those who love God and are called according to his purpose" (Rom. 8:28 NLT). And I know that while most people wouldn't choose their wounds, those who've received God's healing also wouldn't trade them because of the extra measure of love and grace and goodness they've experienced in the mending process.

2. Mission. Your wounds will enable you to see needs that no one else sees and connect with people no one else notices. From your greatest pain will come your greatest purpose. If God allows your heart to be broken, your heart will most likely break for the pain of others. Your suffering won't be wasted. Wait on the Lord; He will reveal an opportunity to redeem your pain by giving you a unique passion for something or someone you might have missed otherwise.

3. Mentorship. God will use your wounds for helping someone who's mending to discover his or her mission. You won't have only your story. You'll become part of someone else's story. That's when your wounds become beauty marks. That's when your pain becomes worth it! You'll see the "goodness of the LORD in the land of the living" (Ps. 27:13). It may seem unimaginable today, but God can do more than you could ever ask or imagine (see Eph. 3:20).

You're going to get to see hope and greater things happen this side of heaven because of what you are going through!

CHOOSE YOUR ENEMY

We each have a choice to make: we can choose to stay isolated, or we can choose to allow our pain to become a beauty mark that moves us to reach out and make a difference in the lives of others.

One thing that helps me choose to serve others is reminding myself who my real enemy is. One day I was standing in my kitchen asking God why He didn't protect my family, when it suddenly dawned on me that my enemy wasn't the drunk driver or the brain injury or the insurance company, or even God Himself. The enemy of my soul and my family was Satan, my accuser and the father of all lies (see Rev. 12:10; John 8:44). I was wrestling not against "flesh and blood" but against the only one who comes to "steal and kill and destroy" (Eph. 6:12; John 10:10). My real battle was with the Devil, and, honey, I was determined to win.

In that moment I decided to channel all my rage and pain into a fight I've been guaranteed to win. I shouted aloud, "Satan, you are gonna pay. You picked the wrong family. You thought you could take us out. But you solidified our purpose, and we are going to spend the rest of our lives making you wish you had left us alone. We are going to tell as many people as we can about Jesus."

Since our family decided to get into the fight of changing lives for eternity, thousands of people have come to faith in Christ and found hope this side of heaven. With the help and accountability of a board of directors, our family started a nonprofit ministry called Hope Out Loud. We travel and speak as a family all over the United States and Canada. God has opened doors for us to share our story at high schools, universities, and churches, with disability groups, and at community-wide events. Hope Out Loud gives hope and resources to families and hurting people all over the world. God has also blessed us with a *Hope Out Loud* radio program, where we encourage listeners and pray Scripture over them. Broadcasts are heard more than eleven hundred times a day in every state in the United States, as well as Australia, Aruba, and Canada. Only God could do that!

Try saying this out loud: "I want to stay in bed and feel sorry for myself." Now try saying, "I want to make Satan pay for messing with me!" Which statement energizes you and gives you purpose? You've got to decide who your enemy is. God isn't your enemy. He wants to redeem your hurts and leverage them for someone else's future. Ask Him to help you do the impossible.

Your pain can turn you inward toward depression or outward toward a new passion. It can give you determination to do things you normally never would have done. Decide today to turn your pain into passion to make a beauty mark on the world!

If you don't feel healthy enough to do that, the next chapter is for you.

Chapter 7

ICE CHIPS, SPONGE VINEGAR, AND LIVING WATER

If I find in myself a desire which no experience in this world can satisfy,
the most probable explanation is that I was made for another world.

C. S. Lewis, *Mere Christianity*

Have you ever been desperately thirsty?

When my dad was in the hospital after heart surgery, he was given nutrition through IVs, but he couldn't have water by mouth for three days. We were so excited that he was alive, and we were expecting his first words when he woke up after surgery to be "I love you!"

Instead, he said, "I'm so thirsty!"

He was craving one drop of water. I'll never forget how happy he was the day he was allowed to have an ice chip.

In the fourth chapter of John's gospel, we read about a Samaritan woman whose soul was craving to be satisfied, like a dry, parched mouth. This woman had developed a bad reputation in her village. The more men she had, the more her soul thirsted for real love.

We're not so different. The more we feed our human desires, the more we want. God made each of us with a soul that is a deep vacuum. Nothing will satisfy the deepest longings of our souls except a relationship with Jesus. God created us this way so that we would search for Him.

Jesus was traveling through Samaria, a town Jews avoided at all costs because of racial hatred. There He had a divine encounter with a Samaritan woman who was an outcast in her hometown. He didn't care what anyone thought about Him. He didn't care what was socially acceptable. Instead, He broke down social and spiritual barriers.

This story makes me fall in love with Jesus all over again.

JESUS WAITED FOR HER

When Jesus arrived at Jacob's well, it was noon and He was physically thirsty and tired from the journey. Jacob's well was a half mile outside the town of Sychar, and it was deep. While His disciples were off fetching lunch, He sat down at the well and waited for someone who might help Him scoop a drink. The Samaritan woman arrived at the well alone at a time when no one else would be there. High noon was too hot for most folks. Imagine her surprise at meeting Jesus, especially when He revealed everything she had ever done and loved her anyway. Jesus knew this woman was scarred and broken. Yet He pursued her and went to the place He knew she would come.

Sometimes in our neediness, we run to Jesus. Other times He runs after us. Often we think we have to get our act together before we can run to Jesus. That isn't true. Jesus forgives us and accepts us as we are.

Have you ever experienced a time when God went out of His way to *pursue* you or tell you that He loves you? Jesus wants to meet you today right where you are.

John narrated this exchange:

> When a Samaritan woman came to draw water, Jesus said to her, "Will you give me a drink?" (His disciples had gone into the town to buy food.)
>
> The Samaritan woman said to him, "You are a Jew and I am a Samaritan woman. How can you ask me for a drink?" (John 4:7–9)

This precious woman couldn't believe that Jesus was speaking to her. A Jewish rabbi would rarely speak to a woman, much less a Samaritan woman. Jews didn't associate with Samaritans because they considered them to be unclean.

Just as He saw the Samaritan woman, Jesus sees you. He stops and notices you. In fact, He's waiting for you to come to Him for help.

Jesus wanted the woman to know whom she was meeting. He explained,

> If you knew the gift of God and who it is that asks you for a drink, you would have asked him and he would have given you living water. (v. 10)

He also told her,

> Everyone who drinks this water will be thirsty
> again, but whoever drinks the water I give them
> will never thirst. Indeed, the water I give them will
> become in them a spring of water welling up to
> eternal life. (vv. 13–14)

The woman thought Jesus was talking about physical thirst, but
He saw past her immediate physical need to the thirst and emptiness
in her heart and soul. He shifted from *everyday* life to *everlasting* life
by making a bold promise that she would *never thirst again*. Only
the Messiah could offer this gift that satisfies the soul's deepest desire.
The same way water is necessary for physical life, salvation is necessary for spiritual life. The big difference is that water satisfies for a
limited time but salvation permanently satisfies; we shall never thirst
again.

The woman wasn't able to understand all the words Jesus spoke.
She said to Him, "Sir, give me this water so that I won't get thirsty
and have to keep coming here to draw water" (v. 15).

Was her soul thirsty for a savior? Did she have scars? Yes! Jesus
revealed to her that she was trying to fill her soul with that which
could never satisfy: she had five husbands and was sleeping with a
sixth man who was not her husband (see vv. 17–18).

Can you imagine how broken, empty, and ashamed she must
have felt? She was running out of options. Who was going to want
her? Yet Jesus offered to give her "living water" (v. 10).

Immediately she demonstrated healing from her shame by going back and speaking to the people she was previously avoiding. Once she had a personal encounter with Jesus, her burden of guilt and shame was lifted.

John shows us what that healing looks like:

> Then, leaving her water jar, the woman went back to the town and said to the people, "Come, see a man who told me everything I ever did. Could this be the Messiah?" (vv. 28–29)

FULL REDEMPTION

This story is so breathtaking, I can hardly stand it! What a stunning illustration of Jesus turning scars into beauty marks. In a few short hours, the Samaritan woman became an evangelist and took the whole town to meet Jesus. Not only did Jesus heal her spiritually with the living water, but He also had a plan and a *purpose* to use her for His glory. This was full redemption! She was transformed from an outcast to a daughter of the King! God used her *because* of her scars, not in spite of them.

In the first century, a woman's testimony wasn't typically valued. However, because of this woman's past and her confession that Jesus had revealed everything she had ever done, the whole town of Sychar was curious enough to walk half a mile out of town to meet Jesus. And many of them believed. In fact, when they urged Jesus to stay with them, He stayed two more days and "many more became believers" (John 4:41).

Does your past ever haunt you? Satan wants to keep you paralyzed and stuck in your past, but God has a new destiny and plan for your future. He wants to redeem your past. Like the Samaritan woman, if you're willing and available, God can use your story to draw others to salvation.

We all have a thirst for significance and purpose. Only an intimate relationship with Jesus can satisfy and fill us up completely. All we have to do is say, "Lord, I'm thirsty." He is the lover of our souls, and He understands our every need and hurt. He experienced more pain than we could ever endure. Even in His last moments on this earth, the Living Water was dying of physical thirst so that we would never be thirsty again.

JESUS CRIED FOR HELP

Jesus was arrested the night before the crucifixion and, presumably, was given nothing to drink after the Last Supper. He was whipped early in the morning, ripping His flesh beyond recognition. He lost blood and, with it, water. By this time His wounds were probably starting to get infected, and He was most likely running a high fever. He had been hanging near suffocation on the cross for six hours—from 9:00 a.m. to 3:00 p.m.—gasping for air through His mouth. Some historians have chronicled that the worst torture of the many tortures of death by crucifixion was the insatiable thirst. One told of a victim who hung for days on the cross and pleaded only for water.[8]

As Jesus hung there writhing in pain, the soldiers were mocking Him and casting lots for His clothes. Finally, Jesus, the Living Water, cried out, "I am thirsty" (John 19:28).

John described what the soldiers did in response:

> A jar of wine vinegar was there, so they soaked a
> sponge in it, put the sponge on a stalk of the hyssop
> plant, and lifted it to Jesus' lips. (v. 29)

Close your eyes and picture being Jesus's mother standing nearby, watching your Son suffering unspeakable wounds and fever, crying out in thirst, and not being able to give him a drink. If I was standing near my son and he was crying for a drink, I would do anything in my power to give him one. The very thought crushes my heart to pieces.

Recently when I was meditating on this horrific scene, tears started streaming down my face and I whispered aloud, "Jesus, I'm so sorry You were thirsty. How can it be that the One who commands the water was willing to thirst for me?"

Jesus was willing to thirst for you too. What great love. What great sacrifice. He wasn't some superhero who was immune to pain. He was human. He felt every wound, even the thirst.

JESUS GIVES US PERMISSION TO ASK FOR HELP

About a thousand years before Christ died on the cross, Psalm 69:21 predicted, "They put gall in my food and gave me vinegar for my thirst." It is utterly remarkable that when Jesus was dying on the cross, gasping for air, He was quoting and fulfilling Scripture. This is one of several scriptures He fulfilled while He was suffering.

It's even more remarkable that the Son of God, who inspired the Scriptures, read the Scriptures, fulfilled the Scriptures, and quoted the Scriptures, also admitted His physical weakness. The great I AM cried, "*I am* thirsty." And when He did, He gave you and me permission to ask for help.

Some of us have trouble asking for help. We might even reason that we think we're being unspiritual or weak in our faith if we admit we need anything but God Himself. Dear friend, God Himself created you to need relationships, to need purpose, to need rest, food, and water. He made you to need many things that quicken your hunger for your greatest need, which is to spend eternity with Him.

Jesus publicly demonstrated His humanity by both asking for physical help and accepting physical help. When someone soaked a sponge in wine vinegar, put it on the stalk of a hyssop branch, and lifted it to His lips, He "received" it (John 19:30).

It doesn't matter how strong you are spiritually, emotionally, or physically—sometimes you'll need to be the hope bearer, and sometimes you'll need to be the recipient. In some seasons of your life, you'll offer help; in other seasons of your life, you'll need to receive it. If the Son of God admitted His need for help, you can too!

JESSIE'S STORY

At age fifty-three, Jessie didn't know she was wounded. She woke up in the middle of the night and thought she was having a heart attack. Her husband called the ambulance, and her midlife "heart attack" turned out to be a panic attack. She continued to have irregular sleepless nights, panic attacks, and shortness of breath, until one morning she could no longer get out of bed. This type-A, ultra-responsible mother didn't get up to take her kids to school and didn't show up for work. It was as though a heavy weight had pinned her down, and she simply couldn't will her body to move. After extensive medical tests, Jessie was ultimately diagnosed with severe clinical depression.

Over the past few decades, Jessie had weathered some significant losses and betrayals. As a strong-willed Christian woman, she had picked herself up by her bootstraps and her Bible and kept right on moving after each blow. She had no idea the battles were chipping away at her soul until her body simply quit functioning. Her physical malfunction was a warning signal that something was wrong beneath the surface.

"I always thought people who claimed to have depression were either fainthearted or overreacting," recalled Jessie. "Now I know it's real. I've had to make some major adjustments in my lifestyle and the way I take care of my body and my mind. Depression actually turned out to be a gift in a way, because it forced me to deal with some painful root issues. My heart had no idea it was wounded, and my mind was too busy to care, but my body was telling a different story!"

Have you ever battled depression? Anger turned inward can lead to depression. There is a mild form of depression called *dysthymia*, where you feel flat all the time, with no emotional highs and lows. Some people can have this kind of depression for years and not even know it. Have you lost interest in normal daily things you used to enjoy? Do you find it hard to be upbeat even on happy occasions? If you answered yes, the remainder of this chapter could change your life.

WARNING SIGNALS

Often we wait until we have physical ailments before we start seeking healing for our emotional wounds. Like the dashboard of a car, our bodies are equipped with numerous warning lights that flash when we need to pay attention to something going on "under the hood" (in our hearts and minds). A warning signal is an alert or alarm that warns us of danger. Some of the warning signals include, but aren't limited to, the following:

- Chronic fatigue
- Anxiety
- Sleeplessness
- Loss of appetite
- Weight loss or gain (usually ten pounds or more)
- Depression (feeling hopeless, helpless, and worthless)
- Suicidal thoughts

If you're experiencing a combination of these physical or emotional symptoms, please seek medical attention.

It's also important to remember that emotions aren't bad; they are God-given warning signals. Denying that you feel sad, angry, or anxious won't solve the root of your problem. Find a trusted friend or counselor who can help you identify your emotions and validate them.

Do you have a close friend you can depend on for encouragement and accountability? Please don't allow yourself to be isolated.

I'm in a texting group with my three best friends. They live in different states, but I can text them anytime my world is falling apart. We don't keep secrets. We know the good, the bad, and the ugly. We love one another unconditionally. We challenge one another to be better moms and wives. We remind one another to stay sexy and flirty for our husbands and to be their girlfriends. My friends are prayer warriors for my family, and they hold me accountable. If you don't currently have a friend you can trust, ask God to bring a treasured friend into your life.

OUT OF BALANCE

Emotions that feel out of control are worth noticing. If you sense that your feelings are running your life, begin to ask smart questions and seek guidance. If there isn't an identifiable medical explanation for your symptoms, that doesn't mean it's time to get tougher. Chances are these alarms are sounding because something is out of balance. You probably need more of something. You might need more water, more exercise, more vegetables in your diet, more sleep, more time with God, more therapy, more community, more boundaries, more vacation, more natural supplements, or more medication.

Maybe you're thinking, *I'm a mom with toddlers; I can't possibly get more rest.* Or, *It would be selfish if I asked for more time to exercise.* But if you have little people depending on you, it's even more essential that you prioritize your health. How much time do you spend on social media? I'm asking myself the same question. If I have time to post pictures and look at my newsfeed, I can find a way to nurture my vitality. One of my favorite ways to relax is to sit in a hot bubble bath and listen to praise music.

My goal isn't to convince you that you need more or less of something. I'm praying for your well-being. Please pay attention to your body's warning signals. Counseling isn't a sign of weakness; it's a sign of strength. When Jesus said, "I am thirsty," He was asking for help. You can do the same.

THOU SHALT TAKE A BREAK

God created our bodies with enough human frailty to need His help. Feelings like thirst, hunger, and fatigue expose the limits of our humanity and remind us daily that we need more of God. If we never got tired or sick or weak, we wouldn't long for God's help. He wove our need for Him into the fabric of our being. In fact, He desires for us to say, "Lord, I'm thirsty for more of You!"

With that frailty comes our need for rest and margin, which means designated space and time to take a break. When God created the world, He modeled margin. After six days of work, He rested on the seventh. God didn't need a rest. He did it to inaugurate a rhythm of rest for the human race that is deficient and dependent on Him. In other words, we need downtime to stop running in circles and be still with Him!

In her book *Rest Assured*, Vicki Courtney says, "We send up a flare prayer for reinforcements to help us *maintain the pace*, never imagining that God wants us to *change the pace*."[9] In fact, we often view our need to slow down the pace as a sign of spiritual weakness.

We falsely assume that the stronger our faith is, the more activity we can handle. But we weren't designed for constant motion. We need uncluttered time to hear God's voice, sit still in His presence, or rest on the couch.

That's why God gave us the gift of margin as one of His top-ten commands. The Sabbath commandment in Exodus 20:8–10, to work six days and then rest one day, was really an issue of trust. We have to trust that Facebook, Instagram, Twitter, and Snapchat will survive without us. Work emails won't spiral into disaster without us. The kids' sports teams will survive for one afternoon without us. It's saying, "God, if I take time out to do what You say to do, I am believing You can take care of things without me better than I can on my own." We exercise trust in God when we practice Sabbath rest.

Often we're so busy taking care of our families that we forget to take care of ourselves. What are you doing to take care of your body and your mental health? A friend of mine recently had to take off a year from work to learn to listen to her warning signals and recover from severe depression. Following is the recovery plan she shared with me after she went back to work. Though your plan may look very different, hers can give you some great ideas for how to intentionally schedule margin and more time for God into your rhythm of living.

What am I doing *daily* to have margin?
- Spending twenty minutes with God
- Exercising for twenty minutes
- Listening to praise music in the car

What am I doing *weekly* to have margin?

- Setting aside one day each weekend for rest and worship
- Turning off all computers and social media for one day
- Taking a long walk outside to pray and hear God's voice

What am I doing *monthly* to have margin?

- Marking off one completely unscheduled weekend
- Getting my nails done
- Having lunch with a friend
- Going on a date with my husband

What am I doing *yearly* to have margin?

- Getting away overnight four weekends a year—two with my husband, one for a women's retreat with friends, and one "alone retreat" with God
- Learning a new hobby
- Going to marriage counseling
- Taking a one-week vacation with no emails

What might your plan for rest look like?

PLAN TO CELEBRATE

If you saw my calendar, you would know that margin is a huge problem for me. When I went to a counselor, the first thing she did was advise me to mark off whole days and weekends on my calendar as downtime to add some breathing room into my schedule. She also advised me to do things that *add* to my "energy bucket" and put boundaries on the things that deplete it. What things energize you, and what things drain you? Take a moment to write out your own plan of what you could do daily, weekly, monthly, and yearly to add healthy margin and energy to your life bucket.

What about scheduling time to celebrate? When was the last time you celebrated a good day? This has been a game changer for me. I put so much pressure on myself to achieve but rarely take time to celebrate. Like scheduling margin in your life, I encourage you to schedule time for celebrating the small victories, such as when your kids get a good grade in school or you have enough money to pay the bills or everyone liked the dinner you made. Take a moment to dance in the kitchen or eat a big chocolate sundae and celebrate.

You can even schedule a whole day of celebration. One of my friends celebrates by staying in her pj's all day and cooking lots of desserts for her family to enjoy. That wouldn't be my idea of a celebration. I would celebrate by spending time with friends, shopping, or having dinner out with my family. Those are all things that add to my energy bucket. How would you celebrate? When you add margin and celebration into your schedule, you'll have more to pour out to others because you've intentionally planned time to keep yourself emotionally healthy.

MORE HEALING AND MORE OF JESUS

Jesus expressing His thirst reminds us that our physical needs lead us closer to discovering our spiritual need. I'm praying that you won't miss one detail of what He accomplished or said on the cross for you. Here's how the apostle Peter explained it in one of his letters:

[Jesus] personally carried our sins
    in his body on the cross
so that we can be dead to sin
    and live for what is right.
By his wounds
    you are healed. (1 Pet. 2:24 NLT)

Jesus is Jehovah Rapha, the almighty healer. He still heals today. He can heal you physically, emotionally, and spiritually.

I had the opportunity to visit Israel recently. This trip was extra-special because Jen was finally healthy enough to travel with me. While we were there, we visited the pool of Bethesda, where Jesus healed a lame man—on the Sabbath! Since physical healing is one of Jen's biggest needs, we decided to pull away from the crowd to pause and pray for her healing there.

It sounds a little crazy, but my husband climbed down to the source of the water and filled a hand-sanitizer bottle with water from the famous pool. (It's the only container we had in our possession.) If you've ever had a child who is suffering, you know you'll try anything to get him or her some relief. It's not that we expected the water to provide some kind of magical healing. For us, it was a symbol of faith. We believed Jesus once stood by this very source of water to heal a man in need. And if He did it then, He could certainly do it again.

After Andy and I prayed, Jen wanted to pray. Much to our surprise, she started sobbing. Since her accident, Jen hadn't been in touch with feelings of sadness. Her voice was one I had never heard before. It was a voice of deep soul pain. It was heart wrenching as Andy and I wept with her, but at the same time, it was a miracle!

Right before our very eyes, God was connecting new pathways in Jen's brain and allowing her to feel emotions of sadness as she cried out for more healing.

For the first time in ten years, Andy and I finally had the moment in time when we could hug and cry with Jen about her brain injury and all she had suffered. In God's grace and mercy, He protected her all of those years from fully comprehending the depth of her injuries. Jen had cried many times because of physical pain, but this was the first time since the accident that she had ever cried out in emotional pain. It was as if God was revealing her emotional frailty for the first time, and as she started to recognize her own need, she cried out for more. Then suddenly her cry for more healing turned into a cry for more of Jesus.

My sister captured Jen's prayer on her iPhone video recorder. It's a treasure we watch over and over. (You can watch the video at Hope Out Loud.)[10] Here are the words she prayed:

Lord, it's such an honor to be here. We're asking for more, Lord. We know You can, Daddy. We know You can. So why wouldn't You, Lord?

Through agonizing sobs she continued,

We need You. You're our hope. You're our purpose. Please touch my body, my eyes, and please heal me from the inside out. Father God, to be anointed with this water means so much. I know there's power in it! Like the miracles You did in the Bible, I know You're not done yet, Lord.

Then she expressed her specific need:

Please, touch my cells and heal the cancer, the thyroid count. Lord, I pray that You would remove the nodule. I know You can do even so much more, Lord. Help my eyes. Heal everything.

Then, in classic Jen style, she praised and thanked God:

Lord, You're our sustainer, and You're my hope. You're the reason I get up in the morning! Thank You for this time. I'm honored. I feel like the luckiest person in the world, and I want to say I love You. I love You. Thanks, Daddy, for listening. It's in Your name, Lord Jesus. Amen.

If God can keep healing Jen, He can keep healing you!

You don't have to travel to Israel to pull away from the crowd and your busy schedule to beg God for more healing and more of Him. Say aloud, "Lord, I am thirsty." Like in the story of the Samaritan woman at the well, our physical thirst leads us to a spiritual thirst. Jesus suffered so you can have more. Ask Him for more today. Like the woman who thirsted for abundant life, crave Jesus! He's the only one who can satisfy the deepest longings of your soul.

Have you ever wondered what God sees when He looks at you? In the next chapter, you'll discover that as a believer, you're clothed with His Son's righteousness. That's how God sees you! God's posture toward His Son, Jesus Christ, is identical to His posture toward you.

Chapter 8

ACCIDENTALLY ACCESSING BILL GATES'S BANK ACCOUNT

*[Christ] has taken our evils upon himself that
he might deliver us from them.*

Martin Luther, *Commentary on the First Twenty-Two Psalms*

When I was a little girl, I discovered a dark spot on my face to the left of my nose. I tried to scrub it, but it wouldn't come off. One day I asked my mom what it was, and she said, "Oh, honey, that's your beauty mark." I believed her, and I was proud to have my own special "beauty mark," until middle school when my friend told me that I had a mole on my face!

If you ask a kindergarten class, "How many of you are great artists?" almost all the kids will raise their hands. If you ask them, "How many of you can sing?" or "How many of you are great at sports?" again, all the hands go up. Ask the same group of kids the same questions seven years later, in the midst of middle school, and almost no one will raise their hands![11] What happened during those seven years? They got hurt. They were wounded. Someone laughed.

Someone said something negative. Someone didn't pick them. Someone said, "That's not a beauty mark; it's a mole!"

Isn't that how life is? We start out thinking we can do anything or be anything. We have big dreams and aspirations until someone tells us we aren't smart enough, pretty enough, or talented enough. Over time we start believing those lies.

Most of us find our worth and value in three things: our appearance, what we do, and what others think about us.

Stop and ask yourself these three questions right now:

1. How do you feel about your appearance?
2. Are you proud of what you do for a living?
3. What do others think about you?

When I was a stay-at-home mom while my kids were growing up, I remember cringing every time I had to fill out paperwork at the school or for a doctor's appointment. I would feel insignificant every time I read the question "Are you employed?" Well, I accomplished lots of things for free. In fact, I was at the school every day: room mom, lunch-duty mom, car-pool mom, Moms in Touch prayer leader (now Moms in Prayer International), youth-ministry gymnastics-team leader, and JV cheerleading coach. But when I had to fill in the blank or check a box to show how I used my time, no one seemed to give credit for all of those things. The only category that described me was "homemaker," and part of me always wondered if anyone would ever know I had other gifts, skills, and dreams.

Now looking back, I realize that "homemaker" was the most fulfilling and rewarding job I ever had. I wouldn't trade it for anything! At the time, though, I was worried about what other people thought of me, or worse, what I thought other people thought of me.

No matter how you answer those three questions, your purpose and significance in life are far greater than what fills in your blanks or what boxes you check. As a follower of Jesus, you are a priceless treasure, a daughter of the King! Your identity is who you are in Christ. No one can take that away from you. It's not about you, what you look like, what you do, or what others think. It's all about Him! We don't have to be what anyone else considers good enough or smart enough or successful enough. We have to accept the truth of what God believes about us. You might be surprised what He actually thinks about you!

TETELESTAI

The last three words Jesus spoke before He died changed history forever. John tells us that "when [Jesus] had received the [wine vinegar], [he] said, 'It is finished.' With that, he bowed his head and gave up his spirit" (19:30).

Three powerful words—"It is finished"—spoken by the most powerful man on the most powerful day in history!

In the Greek, these three words are actually one word, *tetelestai*. It was the word artists spoke after completing a masterpiece. It was the word servants announced after fulfilling their master's mission. Merchants and judges wrote *tetelestai* on debt receipts when they were paid in full. Soldiers shouted this word when victory was declared. And priests used it on the Day of Atonement.

Yom Kippur, the Day of Atonement, was the most important day on the Jewish calendar. It was the day sin was momentarily paid in full by means of a substitute sacrifice under Old Testament law. Leviticus 16 describes the gory details. It required two goats. One was slaughtered in the temple, its blood sprinkled in the Holy of Holies on the mercy seat of the ark of the covenant. This was where God's presence dwelt. The act represented the need to shed the blood of a substitute sacrifice to pay the penalty for sin. Then the sins of the people were confessed over the head of the other goat, which a priest led outside the camp and released into the wilderness to carry the guilt far away. This goat, which became known as a "scapegoat," represented the need for the people's guilt to be transferred elsewhere. One goat paid for sins by its death, and the other was physically expelled to remove the guilt and appease the wrath of God. This complicated ritual was good only for one year. It had to be repeated annually.

I have heard my father, Dr. Ed Hindson, say many times that according to Jewish rabbinic tradition, during the time of Christ, a priest marched the scapegoat outside the city of Jerusalem. Other priests were stationed along the way to relay the call that the scapegoat had been successfully driven out of the city and over a cliff so the guilt could no longer return. From one post to the next, one priest would shout the message to the next priest, "It is finished! It is finished!" *Tetelestai* rang all the way back to the city until the priest at the temple proclaimed one more time that the people's sins had been paid in full.[12] So when Jesus shouted, "It is finished," the word would have been familiar. "It was a shout of triumph, not a whimper of defeat. It was the pronouncement of victory that always came at the end of the Day of Atonement, and every Jew recognized it."[13]

The sacrificial system of the Old Testament was sort of like paying for something with a credit card. What do you do when you have a bill you can't pay for with cash? Most of us swipe a credit card. Your bill with that particular vendor might be paid in full, but soon that credit-card payment is coming due. You have to make at least the minimum payment to satisfy your debtor for the next thirty days. In that sense, you're making payments and accruing debt at the same time. That's how the sacrificial system worked before Jesus came into the world to take care of our sin once and for all.

THE GREAT EXCHANGE

When the sinless Son of God died on the cross for our sins, the sacrifice became permanent. When He proclaimed *"Tetelestai,"* Jesus used the perfect verb tense in the Greek, meaning He was completing an action in the past that would have permanent results continuing in the future. It wasn't like climbing a mountain and saying, "I did it!" It was as if He was saying, "I did it for today, tomorrow, and all of eternity."

That means when you place your faith in Jesus Christ for salvation, instead of your sin being temporarily covered, three *permanent* things happen:

1. Your sin penalty is paid in full.
2. Your guilt is transferred to Jesus.
3. Jesus's righteousness is transferred to you.

This is a game changer! When Jesus willingly sacrificed Himself for us, it wasn't only a substitute punishment—His life for our sin. It was a full exchange—all of Him for all of us. He did more than pay for our sin and take it away. Jesus gave us His right standing with God. He took everything that was wrong about us and exchanged it for everything that was right about Him. The apostle Paul explained it this way: "God made him who had no sin to be sin for us, so that in him we might become the righteousness of God" (2 Cor. 5:21). Jesus traded our sin, sorrow, and pain for His unlimited righteousness, joy, and healing.

Imagine you have an enormous credit-card debt. Go ahead, pick a really big number. Now add a few zeros. How would you feel if you opened your credit-card statement and saw that amount due next week? Now imagine getting another statement and discovering that your debt has been completely paid in full. Except that your balance isn't zero. When your debt was paid, you were also somehow mysteriously linked to Bill Gates's bank account. Now your debt is not only paid in full, but you also have unlimited riches. You traded your debt for his millions. That's a great exchange!

This actually happened to me one time. I went to our bank to make a payment on a business loan. My banker said, "Ma'am, you don't need to make a payment. Your account is paid in full. In fact, the balance is more than four hundred thousand dollars." For a brief moment I thought maybe I had a long-lost benefactor, until the banker and I realized that he was looking at someone else's account!

That's what happens at the point of salvation. God stops looking at your account and starts looking at His Son's account. He wipes out all your debt and credits you with full family benefits. He exchanges your wounds and brokenness for the wholeness and beauty of His Son. In fact, when God looks at you, He sees holiness, purity, and blamelessness because you are clothed with His Son's righteousness.

Everything the Father feels about His Son, Jesus Christ, He feels about you. His Word tells us that He is fully pleased with His Son, so guess what? That means He is fully pleased with you. It doesn't matter what you think about yourself. It doesn't matter what others think about you. It doesn't matter what you think others think about you or even what you think God might think about you. Because of Jesus's work on the cross, everything God thinks about His own Son, He now thinks about you. When Jesus cried, "It is finished," He was trading His identity for yours. That, my dear, is the great exchange!

BEAUTY FOR ASHES

You might wonder, *What exactly do I have to do to keep that righteous status with God?*

The presumption tucked away in that question exposes the great lie of your Enemy. Satan hisses that you can do something to mess up the great exchange, to mar your new identity in Christ, or at least to scar it. Here's the plain truth: there is nothing you did to achieve it, so there is nothing you can do to mess it up.

A few years ago, I read a great book that exposed some lies that had corrupted my identity, propelling me to try to do more and be more for Jesus. It equipped me to believe the truth that there is absolutely nothing I bring to the exchange but brokenness. All I have to do is believe that Jesus's identity is mine. I'm an heir with Him. When I accept the great exchange, there is none of me left to mess it up. It's all Him! In Galatians 2:20, Paul said, "I have been crucified with Christ and I no longer live, but Christ lives in me. The life I now live in the body, I live by faith in the Son of God." I have to repeat that over and over to myself, especially when I'm freshly wounded: "I no longer live, but Christ lives in me."

I meet women all the time who say, "My story is too ugly. It could never be beautiful." I tell them, "It can, if you're willing to trade your story for God's story." In one of the first focus groups I conducted while researching this book, we went around the circle making our wounded statements: *I was abused. I was abandoned. I was betrayed.* When we were almost halfway around the circle, a woman named Courtney offered, "I was the offender. I was unfaithful to my husband with two different men." For a minute we were all shocked. Her confession was unexpected. But then we all started asking her questions. We admired her honesty and wanted to know how she reconciled with her husband. How did she earn back his trust? What was the healing process for God to redeem her story?

Can you think of a time when you knowingly or unknowingly hurt someone else?

The truth is that most of us have been both victims and offenders at some time or another. God can still use your story—no matter how ugly it is. You can trade your story for His!

COURTNEY'S STORY

During our session together, Courtney explained that she can forgive others easily because she knows what she has been forgiven of.

Her husband forgave her and loved her, but it took her several years to regain his trust. They set up ground rules for open communication. Anytime her husband was struggling with her unfaithfulness, he had permission to talk about it, even if it threatened to reopen the wound they shared. Healing was more important to her than hurting. She also put boundaries in place to honor him and give him confidence that she could be trusted. For example, she doesn't "friend" any men on Facebook. She also never allows herself to be alone with another man at a meeting or in a car.

When asked how they healed, Courtney said she would talk aloud to the Enemy and say, "You are not allowed here. I'm no longer a woman involved in sexual sin; I am washed clean" (see 1 Cor. 6:11).

Courtney is now a women's-ministry director at a large church, and she and her husband, who have four children, provide marriage counseling for other couples. They're using their story of pain and reconciliation to help rescue others. Talk about beauty marks! What amazing evidence that God is transforming their wounds into greater purpose. They are trading their ugly story for God's beautiful story of redemption.

Can you relate to Courtney? If you've been the offender, maybe your wound feels as if it's still throbbing within you. Perhaps you're still blaming and condemning yourself. Whether it happened last week or twenty years ago, no wound is beyond God's grace and power.

Courtney has heard *"Tetelestai!"* loud and clear. The complete absolution of her sin in Jesus's "It is finished" has become more real to her than the Enemy's shrewd accusations. The complete forgiveness of her sins has been essential for the healing of Courtney's heart and her marriage.

The way to redemption Courtney experienced is the same way that's open to you as well. Receiving Jesus's "It is finished" in your deep places opens the floodgates for your healing as well. If you haven't yet heard Jesus speaking those three holy words to your heart, today is your opportunity to listen and receive the forgiveness you've hungered for.

CHANGE YOUR THINKING

To trade our stories for God's story, we have to trade our thoughts for His thoughts. My daughter, Jen, shows me every day the power of thinking as God thinks. She says, "God sees my potential. He believes the best about me, so I need to believe the best about myself." Jen is full of peace and joy because she refuses to let negative thoughts consume and control her life.

Like Jen, you can refuse to believe lies and negative thoughts about yourself. Ask God to help you see yourself the way He sees you.

A dear friend said to me recently, "My normal is dysfunction. It's unhealthy thoughts." Can you relate? If you are so broken that you're afraid of being whole, I'm praying for you. I'm claiming over you this promise from 2 Timothy 1:7 (NLT): "God has not given [you] a spirit of fear and timidity, but of power, love, and self-discipline."

Jesus died on the cross and shouted "It is finished" so we could break free from negative thoughts.

GET RID OF THE ANTS

New research shows that negative thinking actually physically damages your brain. You don't have to be in a car accident to injure your brain; you can hurt it by thinking negatively! In *Switch On Your Brain*, Dr. Caroline Leaf gives statistics "confirming that 75 to 98 percent of mental and physical illness comes from one's thought life." Dr. Leaf explains, "*You cannot control the events or circumstances of your life, but you can control your reactions.* And controlling those reactions is the difference between healthy minds and bodies and sick minds and bodies."[14] Psychiatrist Daniel Amen says, "Every thought you have releases chemicals in the brain. Hopeful thoughts release chemicals that help you feel happy and calm. Negative thoughts release chemicals that make you feel stressed and sad."[15]

We choose some of our thoughts and some of them choose us, based on our personalities, past experiences, and present circumstances. Whether we choose to initiate them or are under the attack of our Enemy, we can decide whether to hold on to them or replace them with truth. When we capture a negative thought and replace it with a God thought, we actually create a new neural pathway in our brains that begins healing our brains and our bodies.

According to Dr. Amen, there are three steps we can take to fight the automatic negative thoughts (ANTs) that plague us:

1. Write down your ANTs.
2. Investigate. Are they even true? What triggered them?
3. Talk back. Tell your negative thoughts they aren't true.[16]

One kind of automatic negative thought is personalizing a problem. Instead of saying, "This is a problem," an automatic negative thought would be *I am the problem*. For example, a child who struggles to read in school might think, *I'm stupid. I'm the problem*, instead of thinking, *This is a problem. Reading is hard for me*. Once he isolates the negative thought, though, he can apply to it the truth of what God believes about him: *Reading is hard for me, but I am fearfully and wonderfully made, and I can do all things through Christ*. Whenever he starts thinking, *I'm stupid*, he can talk back to that thought with God's truth and create a new pathway of healing in his brain.

You can too.

When I was a young mom, one of my mentors encouraged me to stop and check every thought. If it didn't line up with the Word of God, she taught me to throw it out and refuse to think about it. This truth is found in 2 Corinthians 10:5: "We demolish arguments and every pretension that sets itself up against the knowledge of God, and we take captive every thought to make it obedient to Christ."

My counselor taught me another way to attack negative thoughts: reality testing. Ask yourself these questions:

1. What is the *worst* thing that can happen?
2. What is the *best* thing that can happen?
3. What is the *most likely* thing to happen?

There is very little in life we can control. Thinking negatively or assuming the worst doesn't give us more control; it actually gives us less control and more stress. When you pick a statement of truth from the Bible and tell it to yourself over and over, you're actually regaining control of your mind, emotions, and physical health. My husband, Andy, used to say every day, "God is going to heal Jen exactly the way He wants her to be." That was the statement of faith he clung to in order to give his mind and body peace.

Recently we were in Atlanta while Jen was having brain therapy sessions with Dr. Jerome Lubbe.[17] He explained to us that your brain believes what you tell it. If you say negative statements to yourself—*I can't get out of bed. Life is hard. I can't do this.*—you will most likely struggle to get out of bed. But if you say positive statements aloud so your brain can hear them—"I am healthy and strong. I'm going to have a great day. I don't want to miss one plan God has for me today."—chances are you will want to get up in the morning. That is why saying positive statements aloud and quoting God's Word aloud over your future is so important. It changes your perspective, and it literally changes how you feel physically.

"BECAUSE I'M WORTH IT"

Your statement of truth could be "Jesus died for me because He thought I was worth it." You could say "Because I am worth it" over and over throughout your day to remind yourself that you are valuable because you're a daughter of the King of Kings and He takes great delight in you. You don't have to let people take advantage of you. As you purpose to change the way you think about yourself, you'll begin viewing yourself the way God views you.

Developing this habit might take some work at first. If it's been hard for you to receive God's grace in every part of your being, spend some time this week sitting with the words of Jesus: "It is finished." Roll them around in your heart and mind the way you'd suck on a piece of hard candy. Luxuriate in them as you would a warm bath. Live with them. Ask God to open the eyes and ears of your heart to receive Jesus's complete forgiveness, grace, and acceptance in a fresh way. As you listen, notice any negative thoughts that bubble up inside you. Write them down and prayerfully offer them to God; then continue to soak in Jesus's announcement: *It is finished.*

COUNTING SCARS

Recently I saw Jen looking in the mirror in her bedroom at the feeding-tube scar on her stomach.

"Hey, babe," I queried, "have you ever wanted to cover up your scars a bit more? Have you ever thought about plastic surgery?"

I expected a simple yes or an indifferent no.

But Jen explained, "Actually, the other day I was counting all the scars on my body."

My eyebrows rose. I bathed that girl's broken body, and even I haven't counted all her scars.

"As soon as I figured out that number," she continued, "God told me that it didn't matter. The number isn't important." She looked right in my eyes to make sure I understood, and then she added, "He didn't want me to focus on the scars."

While I realize it wasn't a typical conversation that every mother has with her young adult daughter, I've come to trust her keen ear for the Lord's voice.

Jen continued, "God told me when He looks at me, He doesn't think, *Oh, she has scars.* He sees His amazing grace."

By this time I'd grabbed a yellow sticky note from Jen's dresser drawer to jot down her words because they were so profound, and I knew a few minutes later she would never remember what she had said.

She explained, "God looks at me and says, 'You are worth it. You are beautiful. You are redeemed. You are priceless. You are chosen.'"

Can you hear in the Lord's assurance to Jen echoes of what Jesus spoke on the cross? He assured Jen that she doesn't need to fix more or do more or be more, because *it is finished.* As Jen and I continued to chat, we agreed that the more scars we have, the greater the Lord's covering is. His grace is enough for every single scar.

That night after our conversation, I lay awake in bed and realized that only four scars count: the ones on Jesus's hands and feet (see Luke 24:39). Those scars gave Him the right to take your wounded heart and proclaim, "It is finished."

My prayer is that today you would be able to look in the mirror, right past your scars, and say, "I am worth it. I am beautiful. I am redeemed. I am priceless. I am chosen."

If you can't do that, it's time to accept the great exchange: trade your identity for Christ's.

Dear one, it's time to stop focusing on what Jesus already declared is finished in the past, present, and future. *Look at His hands. Look at His feet.* He took on your scars and gave you His healing power. What looks like a scar now is being turned into a beauty mark for His glory. You can't undo what He has already done.

Take a minute and go back to the page in your journal where you listed some of your wounds. Then write on top of them "It is finished!"

Chapter 9

PETER, PETER, PETER

Our old history ends with the cross; our new
history begins with the resurrection.
Watchman Nee, *The Normal Christian Life*

The last words Jesus spoke on Earth weren't His dying words; they were His resurrection words. If the words He spoke while He was dying have the power to heal our wounds, the words He spoke after He rose again have the power to transform our wounds into purpose, making them into something beautiful. The cross keeps us from dying; the resurrection gives us a whole new destiny!

WOMAN, WHY ARE YOU CRYING?

If you still aren't convinced that God can redeem your scars and make your story beautiful, Jesus's first resurrection words are for you. The very first person Jesus appeared to when He stepped out of the tomb was a deeply wounded woman, Mary Magdalene. Of all the people who could have borne witness to His resurrection, He chose to appear to the one He had healed and set free from evil spirits. In response, she'd left her home and followed Him.

Luke 8:2 tells us that Mary was possessed with seven demons. People thought she was crazy and treated her as an outcast. No doubt she was mistreated and abused. But when Jesus looked at her, He saw past her physical and emotional scars. He saw the potential of who she was going to become. He recognized a woman who would follow Him and help support His ministry. A woman who wouldn't desert Him or His mother at the cross. A woman who would minister to the early believers. A woman who wouldn't leave her Savior's tomb until she had answers. A woman who would tell her story.

> Now Mary stood outside the tomb crying. As she wept, she bent over to look into the tomb and saw two angels in white, seated where Jesus' body had been, one at the head and the other at the foot.
>
> They asked her, "Woman, why are you crying?"
>
> "They have taken my Lord away," she said, "and I don't know where they have put him." (John 20:11–13)

Jesus's burial had been hurried because of the Sabbath. There was no time to properly mourn or prepare. If you were a woman overwhelmed with grief and fear at the loss of your hero, where would you go? Mary chose to be as close to His body as she could be.

The morning after the Sabbath, very early while it was still dark, Mary went to Jesus's tomb with a few other women. When they arrived and found that the stone had been rolled away, they ran to tell the other disciples that Jesus's body was missing. Peter and John came and saw and wondered and went home. Not Mary. She stayed at the tomb, weeping so hard that she couldn't even recognize who was speaking to her.

> [Then] she turned around and saw Jesus standing there, but she did not realize that it was Jesus.
>
> He asked her, "Woman, why are you crying? Who is it you are looking for?"
>
> Thinking he was the gardener, she said, "Sir, if you have carried him away, tell me where you have put him, and I will get him."
>
> Jesus said to her, "Mary."
>
> She turned toward him and cried out in Aramaic, "Rabboni!" (which means "Teacher").
>
> Jesus said, "Do not hold on to me, for I have not yet ascended to the Father. Go instead to my brothers and tell them, 'I am ascending to my Father and your Father, to my God and your God.'" (John 20:14–17)

Jesus was on His way to heaven to see His Father after enduring the separation from Him on the cross and being in the grave for three days. He had His own all-important agenda at hand. Yet He took time to stop for Mary, the wounded one, who was falling back into utter despair.

"Woman, why are you crying?" He said. It's as if He was asking her, "Do you not know what I have accomplished for you? You will never again be a slave to sorrow or death or sin. I have conquered all of those things!"

Mary didn't recognize Him. Not until He spoke her name. One word. That's all it took. He said it the way no one ever said it before. When other people spoke her common name, they said it in whispers that ignited her shame. "Mary, the girl who had seven demons. Watch out. Here she comes."

When Jesus said her name, His tone was full of compassion and understanding. The kindness in His voice would have communicated to her deep hurting places, "I know what you've been through, Mary. I know how hard it was. I know your soul is fragmented into a million pieces. I'm here to make you whole. I'm here to transform your mess into a beautiful mark on this world. Mary, I have something for you to do. Mary … go tell …"

As I stated earlier, because she was a woman, Mary didn't even qualify as a credible witness. What was she supposed to go tell? Her story. Jesus wanted her to tell what had happened to her. She ran to the disciples and said, "I have seen the Lord!" (v. 18). That was the story she told until her death.

All any of us have to tell is our story. Like Mary, we're called to share what happened to us and how Jesus showed up. Our wounds and scars are the filler details that make other people want to listen, that help others relate. But they're also the very things our Enemy will distort and twist to try to stop us. He can't win, and he knows it. Jesus is walking with you, and He will encourage your heart when you don't think you can take another step.

DON'T STOP SHARING YOUR STORY

I had an experience like Mary's a few years ago as I sat in church on a Sunday morning feeling exhausted and overwhelmed. We had been traveling continuously and telling our story all over the United States and Canada, and we'd come home for Jen to have her thyroid and several lymph nodes removed. I was tormented with worry over how much Jen's cancer had spread. While the pastor was preaching, I was having a conversation in my head with God: *Lord, is it really worth it? Is it worth traveling all over and sharing the gospel? Why does Jen have to suffer again? Why does she have cancer? This is so unfair. I don't think my heart can take much more. Lord, I'm ready to give up!*

At that very moment, someone behind me tapped me on the shoulder and handed me a note written on a piece of yellow notebook paper. As I unfolded the note, my eyes fell on the words "Don't stop sharing your story! Because of your story and your family's testimony, I have given my life to Christ. I have surrendered everything to Him! Please don't ever stop sharing your story!"

Tears began streaming down my face. God loved me enough to answer my question in that very moment. He heard my plea for help and knew how desperate I felt. It was as if Jesus Himself came down from heaven, tapped me on the shoulder, and said to me as He said to Mary, "Woman, why are you crying? Don't stop sharing your story. You are making a difference for eternity! Linda … go tell!"

A young man who was sitting with his wife and children a few rows back had recently finished reading our book *Miracle for Jen* and had taken time to write that note and pass it forward. Wow! God cared about me enough to physically intervene and tenderly address my fears and doubts as I was questioning, "Is it worth it?"

Maybe you're asking that same question. Is it worth it? Yes! God's plans will be far greater than anything you could imagine. They may not be easy, but they will be greater. Don't give up! God will help you one step at a time. This life isn't all there is. God wants to use your story to make a difference for eternity.

Close your eyes and listen to Jesus speak your name, not with shame but with promise, and hear Him say, "Go tell your story!"

EXCUSES

Living in the era of social media, I often find myself looking at other people who are telling their stories, and things appear to work out differently for them than for me. Maybe you're reading this book and thinking, *You can tell your story because it's your daughter. Of course people think it's beautiful. But my story isn't like yours. I have regrets. I caused some of my own wounds. I made poor choices, and I've suffered huge consequences.* That's exactly why God needs you to tell your story. Someone out there needs to hear it! If God has allowed you to survive something painful enough to leave scars, it's because He plans to use it for His purposes. He wants to turn it into a beauty mark.

God might give you the opportunity to share your story with one person or with a group of people at a Bible study or some other gathering. You don't have to be a good speaker; simply be authentic and honest. Share about God's faithfulness and some of the lessons He taught you.

You can always find excuses not to use your story. There will always be obstacles. Here are a few of the most common ones:

- I would tell my story, but not in my hometown or in front of my family.
- I'm not really free to be that authentic.
- I would tell my story, but it would shock people. I'm too ashamed.
- I would tell my story, but I've been disqualified. God can't use me.
- I would tell my story, but it's too painful. I don't ever want to go there again.

If any of these statements sound familiar, Jesus's next resurrection words are for you. A lot of us can relate to Peter's post-resurrection encounter with Jesus.

BACK TO FISHING

After witnessing the empty tomb and seeing the resurrected Jesus twice, Peter didn't go out and start telling his story. In fact, he left Jerusalem and went back north to the Sea of Galilee, where he came from, to go fishing. He went back to his old job, to who he was before he met Jesus. You'd think that Peter, the brash, bold disciple, would be running around telling everyone what he had seen. But he wasn't.

If you had seen a dead man alive and walking, would you go fishing? You might if you had something to be ashamed of. Or if you felt disqualified. Or if you were afraid of facing the pain of your past. Then you might hide behind something safe and normal like fishing.

The last time Peter had seen Jesus before His death wasn't an encounter to be proud of. In fact, it was Peter's greatest personal failure. He had promised to follow Jesus and fight for Him to the death. But when the soldiers came to arrest Jesus, Peter got scared and abandoned Him, watching Jesus on trial from a distance.

John 18:18 (NLT) says, "Because it was cold, the household servants and the guards had made a charcoal fire. They stood around it, warming themselves, and Peter stood with them, warming himself." Three times people standing near the charcoal fire asked Peter if he knew Jesus, and three times he emphatically denied it. After the third denial, Jesus turned and looked at him. That was the last time Peter had looked Jesus in the eyes. Peter ran away in shame, hid, and was nowhere to be found during the crucifixion.

Have you ever been ashamed of your actions and tried to hide from God? I have. The irony is that no one can hide from God. He sees you, and He will pursue you because He wants to restore His relationship with you.

After the resurrection, Mary was thrilled Jesus was alive and told everyone what she had seen. Peter had seen it too, but he chose to go fishing.

Yet Jesus saw past what Peter had done and recognized the potential of who he could become in the future. Jesus wanted to reinstate him.

Peter had been fishing all night without catching a single thing when Jesus repeated the miracle He performed when He first called

Peter to join Him as a follower. Jesus called out to him from the shore, "Throw your net on the right side of the boat and you will find some [fish]" (John 21:6). When Peter tried the other side, the nets were so full of fish that he couldn't get them back in the boat.

Immediately Peter knew that Jesus had come back for him. He remembered this very same miracle Jesus had performed in the past. Peter dove into the water and swam to shore in his clothes to meet Jesus once again face-to-face.

That's when Peter saw it. The *charcoal* fire. It's a distinct smell. How could he miss it? Even though charcoal fires were common in that culture, the words "charcoal fire" appear only twice in Scripture, once when Peter denied Jesus and again in this moment when Jesus pursued him. Do you think that was a coincidence?

Our memories are triggered by our five senses. Peter's mind probably flashed back to the last charcoal fire. He may have been thinking, *Jesus isn't happy to see me. He came to remind me that I failed Him.*

"DO YOU LOVE ME? FEED MY SHEEP."

A closer look at this scene reveals that Jesus had no interest in shaming Peter.

> When [the disciples] got [to shore], they found breakfast waiting for them—fish cooking over a *charcoal fire*, and some bread.
>
> "Bring some of the fish you've just caught," Jesus said. So Simon Peter went aboard and dragged

the net to the shore. There were 153 large fish, and yet the net hadn't torn. (John 21:9–11 NLT)

Peter saw the charcoal fire, and instead of embracing Jesus, he turned aside to go count fish. It appears he was avoiding Jesus again. How else did John know there were 153 fish? Peter went and counted the fish before he returned to eat breakfast with Jesus.

"Now come and have some breakfast!" Jesus said. None of the disciples dared to ask him, "Who are you?" They knew it was the Lord. Then Jesus served them the bread and the fish. This was the third time Jesus had appeared to his disciples since he had been raised from the dead.

After breakfast Jesus asked Simon Peter, "Simon son of John, do you love me more than these?"

"Yes, Lord," Peter replied, "you know I love you."

"Then feed my lambs," Jesus told him.

Jesus repeated the question: "Simon son of John, do you love me?"

"Yes, Lord," Peter said, "you know I love you."

"Then take care of my sheep," Jesus said.

A third time he asked him, "Simon son of John, do you love me?"

Peter was hurt that Jesus asked the question a third time. He said, "Lord, you know everything. You know that I love you."

Jesus said, "Then feed my sheep." (vv. 12–17 NLT)

After breakfast Jesus spoke to Peter face-to-face. He didn't condemn him. Jesus evoked Peter's painful memories of betrayal—denying Jesus three times—to give him an opportunity to have victory over his failures. Jesus gave Peter a chance to declare "I love you" for each of his denials. Do you see what Jesus was doing? Beside another charcoal fire, He restored Peter. It's as if Jesus was saying, "It's okay, Peter. I know your weakness and shame, but I still want you to feed My sheep. Together, we're going to replace all of those painful memories with victory!"

Dear friend, if God is calling you back to face your painful past, it isn't to harm you. It's to set you free. He wants to replace your tragedy with triumph. It's time to redeem your ruins and change your destiny. He is gentle, and He won't take you back there until you're ready. But you can be sure that when He does, it's because He wants to heal you. And if He heals you, you can be sure it's because He wants to use you. He is getting you ready to tell your story.

Jesus told Peter, "Feed my sheep." That was Jesus's way of saying, "Share My gospel message! Tell your story!" Peter went back to Jerusalem, the very place where he had denied Jesus three times, and shared his story on the day of Pentecost. Guess what? Three thousand people believed his story and found new life in Jesus Christ! God redeemed the ruins of Peter's life a thousand times over. One thousand people were saved for each denial. That's a beauty mark! Peter was no longer a coward. He became the brave leader of the early church. He no longer used his words to deny Christ. He used them to proclaim Christ. And he started in the very place where he had failed.

God wants to restore you at the point of your failure. The cross offers you forgiveness, but the resurrection offers you *full restoration*.

That means that if you fail in your parenting, God doesn't only offer you grace and forgiveness; He also wants to restore you to be a great parent. If you fail in your marriage, guess how He wants to use your story? To help restore marriages. If you were abused, guess how He wants to use your shame? To rescue others from shame. If you've been wounded by loss, guess how He wants to use your grief? To help others find eternal hope in Him.

Any story becomes beautiful when it reveals God's handiwork. It doesn't matter how ugly and painful your past is, God can use it all for His glory. He will take every broken piece and make it into His masterpiece.

GOD IS THE AUTHOR OF MY STORY

Last week I was sitting on our back porch with Jen. She was drinking her favorite chai tea, and I was sipping on my vanilla latte. In the quietness of the moment, I asked her how she felt about her life.

She quickly replied with a smile, "My story is God's story. He is the author. I didn't want a brain injury, but I wanted to be different. I wanted to shine and be passionate for Jesus."

"Yes, Jen, I know you wanted to shine." But I probed deeper: "Have you ever been angry at God for the pain and suffering you've endured?"

"No," Jen replied with childlike faith. "Before my brain injury, I was too shy to pray out loud and I was begging God for boldness. Now I have the courage and strength I always wanted. I'm so honored God would use me."

I continued probing her. "What about your scars? You used to tell me you wanted to erase them."

"I know," Jen admitted. "I used to be ashamed of my scars. Not anymore. Now I'm proud of them. My scars help me tell my story. People question my thyroid scar on my neck the most, especially little kids. It's cool because I can share the hope of Jesus. How He loves me. How He cares for me."

"Jen, you always have a positive attitude, which is great." Then I nudged further: "But don't you ever question why God hasn't healed your vision and your memory? Does it ever make you sad that you can't drive a car? Don't you sometimes wish you could have your own apartment or remember what you did last week?"

Jen thought for a moment, and then she said, "Well, I believe God is still healing me. He isn't finished yet. He whispers to my heart that the best is yet to come and that someday I'll understand. So I trust Him."

Sometimes I'm envious of Jen's freedom. It's as if she doesn't have the cares of this world.

She took another sip of her chai, and then she said, "We all have a different story. When we get to heaven, God is going to ask us, 'What did you do with the story I gave you? Was it all about you or all about Me? Did your story reflect My name?'"

As if that wasn't enough wisdom for one day, suddenly a huge smile spread across Jen's face, and she giggled with joy. "I want to reflect Jesus. My prayer is that I would shine with a hint of God's glory!"

GO AND MAKE DISCIPLES

You can be sure Jesus saved the best words for last. If you knew you were leaving the people you loved dearly and wouldn't see them again for a very long time, don't you think you'd be very intentional about your last words? The very last resurrection words Jesus spoke on this earth before He ascended to heaven are famously known as the Great Commission:

> Therefore go and make disciples of all nations, baptizing them in the name of the Father and of the Son and of the Holy Spirit, and teaching them to obey everything I have commanded you. And surely I am with you always, to the very end of the age. (Matt. 28:19–20)

Millions of sermons, speeches, and books have been written about these last words of Jesus. Churches, nonprofits, and ministries have been born out of this command. Basically, the Great Commission can be boiled down to a command and a promise:

Command: Go and tell your God story!
Promise: I will be with you always.

Do you think the ragtag group of uneducated fishermen, tax collectors, and prostitutes first hearing these words ever thought they would travel to the ends of the earth to tell their stories? God used their stories to start a movement that is still active nearly two thousand years later. He wants your story to be a part of it today.

You may go to the end of your street; the end of your town, where no one else wants to go; across the country; or across the globe via the Internet or an airplane. Jesus's promise is always the same: I will be with you. I will use you in ways you never dreamed possible. I will take everything ugly about you and repurpose it for My glory.

Who ever would have thought that God could use a little fifteen-year-old girl who was too scared to pray out loud? God allowed her to be wounded, and in the healing process, He gave her a new story. He is taking the very injury I thought would end her life and is using it to help others find new life.

After Jen and I chatted over chai tea and a vanilla latte, it finally dawned on me—God not only chose Jen; He also chose *me*. He chose me to be her mom, and He chose our whole family to help her share the hope of Jesus with anyone who will listen.

I SEE BEAUTIFUL

Every day I make the choice to be either bitter or better. To see scars or beauty marks.

Even though my physical and emotional scars are still painful, God is redeeming everything I've suffered and is using me for His glory.

That's your story too. Your scars are being transformed into beauty marks in the hands of your Savior.

This is a prayer I've prayed for you that includes prophetic words about Jesus, but since you're His daughter, you also can claim these words and ask God to use your story to bring healing and new life to others:

The Spirit of the Sovereign LORD is upon me,
   for the LORD has anointed me
   to bring good news to the poor.
He has sent me to comfort the brokenhearted
   and to proclaim that captives will be released
   and prisoners will be freed.…
To all who mourn …,
   he will give a crown of beauty for ashes.
   (Isa. 61:1, 3 NLT)

Now go and tell your story. Make your beauty mark!

Chapter 10

WOUNDED WOMEN WANTED

Other people are going to find healing in your wounds.
Your greatest life messages and your most effective
ministry will come out of your deepest hurts.
Rick Warren, *The Purpose Driven Life*

As Jen slowly began to emerge from her coma, our insurance was threatening to send her home from her rehabilitation hospital because she wasn't progressing fast enough.

Then one night, around midnight, I got a call from my friend who was staying in the hospital with Jen because I was still too injured to stay all night with her.

She said, "Linda, I hated to wake you up, and at first I thought I was dreaming, but you won't believe what Jen is doing! She has been praying out loud for over an hour. It's like she is in the very presence of God, and she isn't asking for anything. She is worshipping and praising Him! I think she is sitting at the feet of Jesus!"

This was the same child who could barely speak one word in speech therapy hours earlier. Several of our friends and family saw this miracle. Many of her nurses and therapists were witnesses too.

Jen's body and soul were broken, but her spirit wasn't. It was alive and whole and fully functioning! In fact, her doctors started recommending that we take her praise music with us to therapy so she could progress faster!

I realize this isn't everyone's experience emerging from a coma, but this was Jen's experience. I feel as though we got to glimpse the true power of God's Spirit at work in us while her spirit was accentuated. Jen is still stronger in her spirit than in her soul and body, which is one of many beautiful gifts the accident gave us. However, as her mind, emotions, will, and body started to heal, it got harder for her to function fully in the Spirit. The more aware she was of the outer world, the more frustrated she became. That's when she started quoting Scripture aloud constantly.

I believe her spirit was fighting to stay strong as her soul and body were growing stronger. That's how we came to have a ministry called Hope Out Loud, because Jen was continually proclaiming the hope of God and His Word out loud day and night. Jen's woundedness didn't disqualify her from being used by God. Instead, it superqualified her.

POWER IN WEAKNESS

It seems that the more broken our souls and bodies are, the more desperate we are to rely on the Spirit for survival. I want you to be encouraged that even if you feel spiritually weak, in Jesus your spirit is whole. Your soul or body may still be very wounded and broken, but you are exactly where you need to be in the healing process! Your brokenness is a gift in God's hands. In fact, it's the very thing that makes the Holy Spirit obvious and strong in you. The stronger our souls and bodies are, the more likely we are to rely on them. The weaker our souls and bodies are, the more likely we are to engage the Spirit's help.

On the days when I'm discouraged, Jen will say to me, "Mom, you need a brain injury! Your problem is that your brain gets in the way and you think too much. You need to let go and trust God!"

Remember when God told Paul, "My power is made perfect in weakness" (2 Cor. 12:9)?

Paul got excited and replied, "That is why, for Christ's sake, I delight in weaknesses, in insults, in hardships, in persecutions, in difficulties. For when I am weak, then I am strong" (v. 10).

I want to convince you that your wounds can work to your advantage. Your Enemy meant them for evil, but God is using them as the very thing that makes His Spirit grow stronger in you! If your soul is a hot mess, that mess may be the very thing that brings you back to Jesus. If He fixed your soul as soon as you came to Him, you wouldn't need Him anymore. You might not seek Him so desperately. You might miss most of what He has planned for you.

Your body and soul may be screaming out that they need a quick fix, but your spirit knows that what you need is more of Jesus. He will help you untangle the mess! Yes, it may take some time and hard work. It may not always be fun or easy, but Jesus will help heal your brokenness one step at a time.

BECOMING GOD'S MASTERPIECE

A masterpiece takes time to perfect. It's a process that requires perseverance. Not only is God in the process of healing our wounds, but

He also has a plan to use us to accomplish good things for Him and His kingdom. I love the promise God gives us in Ephesians 2:10: "We are God's masterpiece. He has created us anew in Christ Jesus, so we can do the good things he planned for us long ago" (NLT).

All three Synoptic Gospels mention a woman who'd lived twelve years with a blood disease (see Matt. 9:20–26; Mark 5:25–34; Luke 8:43–48). When she touched the hem of Jesus's garment, she was healed. Jesus made her body well in an instant, but don't you imagine she would have had hidden emotional wounds in her soul that needed healing too? I'm sure she had good days and bad days as she continued to live in a broken world.

Do you ever feel too dirty or unclean to come to Jesus?

This woman with an issue of blood was an outcast in her village, not because of any sin she had committed but because her disease made her ritually unclean. Under the Mosaic law (see Lev. 15:25–27), anyone who touched her or touched anything she sat on or lay on would be considered ceremonially unclean. She couldn't even go to the temple. Maybe you can relate to her at some level because you tried to go to church and felt as though your presence made others uncomfortable. Perhaps you even felt unworthy or unwanted.

It's hard to imagine how isolated, humiliated, and unloved she must have felt. For twelve years she'd suffered with this incurable disease that caused constant pain and drove her into poverty. I can't even imagine not being welcomed to touch people for twelve years. It makes me want to cry just thinking about it. Touch is a basic need we all have.

I suspect this woman was trying to move through the crowd unnoticed. She was probably covering her face with a shawl. By law, she knew that if she touched Jesus, it would make Him ritually unclean. But she also believed He was the one person who could heal her. She was desperate! He was her only hope, and she was willing to take the risk.

It appears that she didn't want Jesus to identify her, because she touched the hem of His garment from behind. Immediately Jesus felt the power go out of Him, and He said, "Who touched my clothes?" (Mark 5:30).

I believe Jesus wanted to acknowledge her in front of the crowd. He wasn't ashamed that an unclean woman touched Him. His healing power was greater than her sickness.

She came trembling and fell at Jesus's feet, acknowledging that she was the one who had touched Him. Jesus looked at her with compassion and replied, "Daughter, your faith has healed you. Go in peace and be freed from your suffering" (v. 34).

This is huge! Jesus addressed her with affection and endearment, calling her "Daughter." It's the only time He used this word in the Gospels. He spoke to her intimately as if she were the only person in the crowd.

He stopped. He noticed her. He spent time with her. He wasn't too busy for her.

I believe Jesus wanted the crowd to know she was healed to restore her honor and identity in front of everyone. She had a hidden wound, like a scar hidden under her clothing or in her heart. What if people didn't believe she was healed and still shunned her? Jesus made sure everyone knew she was clean. He turned her wound of pain and humiliation into a beauty mark.

This woman risked everything—public rebuke and possible punishment—because she believed that Jesus could heal her. Don't be afraid to reach up and touch Him through prayer. His healing power is still available to us today.

Your heavenly Father wants you to be healed. He delights in seeing you live abundantly and full of joy. The process is continuous and does require intentional effort on your part. At the same time, your Abba Father will help you and will never leave you or forsake you (see Heb. 13:5).

SHE IGNITED FAITH IN OTHERS

My favorite part of this story is what happened later in the sixth chapter of Mark's gospel. Word traveled fast about the woman who touched the fringe of Jesus's garment and had been healed immediately. Her testimony ignited faith in many others, and they brought all their sick friends to Jesus:

> Wherever he went—into villages, towns or countryside—[people] placed the sick in the marketplaces. They begged him to let them touch even the edge of his cloak, and all who touched it were healed. (6:56)

When you're wounded and you trust God, it sparks a flame in others. People are watching how you respond to suffering and pain. Your faith can encourage others to believe and trust God for the impossible! The faith of the woman who touched Jesus's garment still moves me today as I read her story. It makes me want to believe that Jesus can do more to heal the broken places in my life.

Once you've reached out and touched Jesus and had part of you made right, you'll know deep down in your soul, it's only the beginning of what He can do.

On the wall of my kitchen is a picture of a modern-day girl in jeans and tennis shoes touching the hem of Jesus's garment. At the bottom of the picture are the words "… and all who touched him were healed" (Mark 6:56 NLT). Every day my daughter stops at this picture and talks to Jesus. She tells Him how much she loves Him, and she praises Him in advance for more healing.

One day she was jumping up and down like an exuberant child, and I said, "What are you doing?"

Jen replied joyfully, "God is speaking to my heart, and He isn't done healing me yet. He is still healing my brain!"

I pray that her confidence, like the confidence of the woman with an issue of blood, sparks a flame of hope in you today.

MIGHTY WOMEN WITH WOUNDS

Last year I met with a small group of women to talk about releasing pain. Afterward, one of the women handed me a napkin with her résumé of pain scrawled in ballpoint pen. It was shocking. It read like this:

Incest, age 12
Rape, age 14
Parents divorced, age 15
Mom depressed, age 16
Ran away from home, age 16

Teenage pregnancy, age 18

Disowned by my family, age 18

In an abusive relationship, age 19

Baby's dad in prison for drug addiction, age 20

Two miscarriages, ages 25–30

Porn addiction in marriage, age 31

Desire to divorce, age 32

At first I felt devastated for her. How could one woman survive such pain? I hugged her, and we sat and prayed together. We asked Jesus to come to her rescue and heal her a little more each day. Then suddenly I felt hope springing up inside me, and a smile spread across my face. I looked at her napkin and said, "It looks like you belong in the line of Christ!"

God's plan to bring salvation into the world hinged on the faithfulness of wounded people. Only five women are mentioned in the ancestry of Christ in Matthew 1, and when you read their stories, you'll see they had all suffered wounds. They all had very different wounds, yet God chose to place them in the royal line of the King of Kings. Normally we think of a royal bloodline as pure and flawless, yet God specifically chose to use these wounded women in the lineage of His Son. It's a beautiful picture of how God redeems all our hurts and repurposes them in greater ways than we could ever imagine.

As I continued to pray for the woman who had handed me that napkin, the Spirit ignited my heart and mind to notice the very particular ways God had used wounded women to accomplish His purposes in the lineage of Christ.

Tamar

Tamar suffered great loss when her first two husbands died, leaving her childless. According to the custom of that day, Tamar's father-in-law, Judah, was supposed to give her his third son in marriage to provide a son that would be an heir of his inheritance and provide for her. Judah told Tamar to go back home and live with her parents until the third son was old enough to marry her. But Judah was afraid his third son would die too, so he betrayed Tamar and never gave her the third son to marry. After Judah's wife died, Tamar disguised herself as a prostitute, tricking her father-in-law into sleeping with her. Judah was going to have her burned to death because he believed she had become pregnant through prostitution, until she proved to him that the baby was his. Judah granted her mercy, and God gave her twin sons to replace her lost husbands (see Gen. 38; Matt. 1:3).

Rahab

Rahab's father probably rented her out as a prostitute for money because they lived on the outer wall of Jericho, where the poorest people lived. Yet she feared God and hid the Israelite spies. Because of her faith, not her goodness, God spared her house alone when the walls of Jericho fell. She saved her whole family from death and married a respectable Hebrew man. God chose her to be in the line of Christ even though she wasn't an Israelite (see Josh. 2; 6:25; Matt. 1:5).

Ruth

Ruth's husband, brother-in-law, and father-in-law all died. Ruth, a Moabite girl, was a widow at a young age, yet she chose to leave her home country and stay with her mother-in-law when Naomi returned to Bethlehem, even worshipping Naomi's God. Because she refused to leave Naomi, Ruth was destined to be an outsider and a pauper in a foreign land. Yet God provided a husband named Boaz to rescue Ruth, and she became the great-great-grandmother of King David (see Ruth 1–4; Matt. 1:5).

Bathsheba

Bathsheba is usually remembered as an adulterous woman, but we don't know for certain whether she did anything to deliberately entice King David. Bathsheba was bathing at a time when all the men were supposed to be off at war. In the meantime, King David, who ordinarily would have been with his army, saw her from his roof and called for her. She likely couldn't refuse the king's advances. When Bathsheba became pregnant, David had her husband, Uriah, killed to cover up his sin. Bathsheba may or may not have known about David's plan to murder her husband. Soon afterward, she suffered the heart-wrenching pain of her baby son dying. Then in God's great mercy, He gave David and Bathsheba another son, Solomon, who eventually became the wisest and wealthiest king on Earth (see 2 Sam. 11–12; Matt. 1:6).

Mary

Mary, the mother of Jesus, would have endured gossip and rejection from her family and friends, who likely assumed that she had sex before marriage, violating the law. She would have been an outcast in her hometown.

Joseph knew the child wasn't his, and according to Jewish law, he could have had Mary stoned to death. Instead, he planned to divorce her quietly. She would have been shamed and condemned by the people in her hometown, yet she was innocent. After the angel appeared to Joseph, he took her as his wife. Years later, she watched as her innocent Son, Jesus, was rejected, mocked, and beaten, and then died on a cross. She must have suffered from a broken heart in ways we can't even imagine. Yet she birthed the Savior of the world (see Matt. 1:18–25; Luke 1; John 19)!

As I drove home from that gathering of women who were brave enough to face their wounds, I continued to pray for the woman who had handed me the napkin. As I did, I realized, *I bet everyone in the line of Christ was wounded.* I mean, we've kind of established the fact that if you're breathing, you're wounded. I bet these women weren't remembered by name because of their wounds. Everyone has wounds. My hunch is that they were remembered by name *because of their healing.* If you have time to read their full stories, you'll discover that each one experienced a measure of healing.

Their stories remind us that healing is possible.

Tamar's pain gave her not one but two sons—twins. Rahab's pain gave her a powerful purpose and an escape from her former life of prostitution. Ruth's pain gave her a love relationship with the one true God and a man who was a respected spiritual leader. Bathsheba's pain enabled her to raise the wisest man who ever lived. Mary's pain brought salvation and healing to the world. These women aren't known for their wounds; they've been remembered for their healing!

Healing is possible when we run into the arms of Jesus.

He is waiting for you to come and ask Him for what you need today. Do you need to feel His love? Do you need to be filled with His peace? Ask Him. Be still and listen to what He speaks to your wounded heart. These words in Jeremiah fill me with great hope: "'Why do you cry out over your wound, your pain that has no cure? … I will restore you to health and heal your wounds,' declares the LORD" (Jer. 30:15, 17).

As you continue the healing process and allow the words of Jesus on the cross to guide you, it's important for you to believe that God can and will use you the way He used the mighty women in the lineage of Jesus. The voice of the Enemy hissing that you're unqualified—because of the life-altering circumstances you couldn't avoid or the ones you could—isn't trustworthy. Instead, God longs to use you to touch the lives of others. Not only are you qualified, but God will use you in *greater ways* because of the wounds and pain you've endured.

SARAH'S STORY

Sarah was abused as a child and grew up in a broken home.

After hearing Jen and me speak in Florida, she asked if we could grab lunch before we flew home. As we sipped tomato soup, she confessed, "Linda, my scars are still so painful. There is nothing beautiful about them."

I already knew that she had purchased an old house and launched a ministry to welcome and shelter teens from the street, feeding them, clothing them, and offering them a place to sleep.

I looked at her and said, "Sarah, your pain has motivated you to reach out and help teenagers who are hurting and don't have parents who care about them. These kids have no one they can trust. You understand their wounds, and God has given you a special ministry to feed, clothe, and love on them."

A glance at her face suggested that Sarah was weighing my words, deciding whether to trust them.

I continued, "Your scars have become beautiful, and you didn't even know it. Your pain has a purpose. It makes you passionate to help others and ignites a strong desire within you to meet the needs of these wounded teenagers."

Yes, the wounds from Sarah's past had left painful scars, but I wanted her to know that scars aren't ugly when they represent healing—and when God uses them to heal others. Sarah continues to help teenagers who feel abandoned and alone. They can stay in the teen shelter for days or weeks if they need a place to sleep. She teaches them about God's unconditional love and how to pray and read God's Word. Sarah, along with volunteers she's trained, helps them find jobs to support themselves.

Leveraging your scars to help someone else heal is beautiful. What if your story could reach someone with hope whom no one else could reach? Your pain can become your ministry. Your mess can become your message. You can move from victim to victor. The world needs your scar story! God will orchestrate the audience as you engage a neighbor, coworker, family member, or church group. Or perhaps God will open doors for you to share with thousands. Regardless, you can make an impact one person at time. Your scars don't always have to be associated with pain. They can become beauty marks, living proof that something painful in the past was healed. Proof that someone else can heal too.

A NEW WAY OF SEEING

Five months after our car wreck, I was sitting in our oversize chair with my daughter, Jen. Her vision was impaired because of her brain injury, and it was the first time she was close enough to be able to see the scar on my face. Because of the cortical blindness she'd suffered as a result of her brain injury, she could see only a little bit of the world at a time. I'll never forget what she said to me.

"Mom," she cooed with compassion, "I wish I was hurt instead of you!"

As tears streamed down my face, I responded, "Oh, honey, I'm the one who worries about you."

Jen joyfully exclaimed, "Don't worry about me. Anything that happens to me is in God's hands!"

She had absolutely no idea that she'd been so close to losing her life. Or that she'd had to relearn how to swallow and talk and walk. At that moment Jen was still surviving on a feeding tube and had no short-term memory. She didn't even know she was injured. She had scars all over her body, but she hadn't yet discovered them when she first noticed mine. She would never again be a normal teenager. She'd never return to cheerleading or soccer, get a driver's license, or go away to college.

Though I was mourning every one of her losses, she was content with nothing but Jesus. It was the one thing she always held in her awareness. Jen trusted Him completely. She was consistently joyful, praising God and talking to Him constantly out loud.

Over the next year, as God continued healing Jen little by little, she started to become aware of her scars. She didn't like them. My eleven-year-old son, Josh, was different. He was proud of the scars on his nose and above his left eye because he was getting tons of attention at school, and all the girls loved him. But like other more typical teens, Jen had begun to wish her scars would go away. Day after day, she asked me questions about them. I often heard the same questions over and over.

One day I said to her, "Jen, we don't have scars, we have *beauty marks*. Our beauty marks help tell our stories and shout to the world that God is faithful and is healing us every day."

Because Jen didn't have a short-term memory, I didn't know if she'd retain the lesson.

A few days later, though, Jen was marching around our kitchen exclaiming, "I'm gonna have a ministry to the world! I'm going to use my beauty marks to help people all over the world find hope and healing."

I was thinking, *Jen, you are so confused. You can't even find the bathroom. How are you going to help people all over the world?*

Today, after telling our story for ten years, writing books translated into six other languages, producing a radio program heard in fifty states and three other countries, and offering thousands of people hope and healing, just as Jen predicted, I still marvel at what God has done with our mess.

Jen often says, "All of our pain would be worth it if one life was saved."

GOD WANTS TO USE YOUR WOUNDS TOO

Like our family and the women in the lineage of Jesus, your greatest ministry will develop out of your wounds. When you look around, what problems do you see? Who needs your help? Whom could you comfort? Your wounds give you passion and purpose. Take a moment to pray and ask God to use your wounds to help others.

Paul described this process best when he penned these words: "Praise be to the God and Father of our Lord Jesus Christ, the Father of compassion and the God of all comfort, who comforts us in all our troubles, so that we can comfort those in any trouble with the comfort we ourselves receive from God" (2 Cor. 1:3–4).

Your wounds don't disqualify you from blessing others. God can use you to help others before you're completely whole. The truth is that some of our physical and emotional wounds will never be completely whole until we get to heaven. The goal while we're on this earth is to experience God's daily healing and to be available for Him to repurpose our wounds for His glory.

In the next chapter, you'll learn to access relief for your broken, hurting places that will help you win the daily battle for your heart and mind and continue healing.

Chapter 11

P IS FOR POWER

The victory is greater than the suffering.

Jen Barrick

When the drunk driver hit us head-on going eighty miles per hour, I was sitting in the front passenger seat of our Sienna van. As a result of the collision, the front dashboard and middle console smashed up against me, encasing my body and crushing my whole left side. The radio controls were all the way up to my chest. Broken ribs on my left side caused my left lung to collapse. The bones in my left arm and foot were crushed into so many pieces, they could never heal on their own. The first thing doctors did the morning after our accident was insert metal plates into these broken places to provide some immediate strength and stability for all my fragile pieces. In time my pieces began to grow back together because they were attached to something sturdy and whole.

Offering you a sturdy support for daily living is the purpose of this chapter. I want you to be able to access practical relief for your broken, hurting places moment by moment. So we'll insert some "metal plates" where you need them most to give you a firm foundation as you continue your healing journey.

If your dreams have been shattered and if you're still struggling to make sense of the brokenness God has allowed, this chapter is for you.

TUG-OF-WAR

Your soul is the battlefield in what might be compared to a spiritual tug-of-war. Your spirit—the part of you that connects to God—and your body are at war for your soul, which comprises your mind, will, and emotions. If you're alive in Christ, you have a fixed spirit living in a broken body and soul that are bumping up against a lot of other broken bodies and souls. Wounds are inevitable. When your soul gets crushed in the battle of life, the immediate goal of healing is *not* to fix your soul. That will take some time because there are so many fragile pieces. The immediate goal of healing is to strengthen and secure your spirit. As your spirit becomes stronger, your soul will begin to align with your spirit, and healing will unfold over time.

It sounds simple. But the tug-of-war for our souls is a raging battle. Our flesh wants us to soothe the wounded places by patching and protecting and escaping the pain. Of course it's our natural tendency to self-medicate. Often we turn to addictions, isolation, denial, rebellion, food, or even shopping to make us feel better. I like to drown out my sorrows with a bag of chips and sour cream. Our bodies scream for a quick fix in the broken places.

The best advice I could ever give you as a friend and fellow wounded soul is to stop trying to fix what is broken and run toward solid ground. Start by strengthening what is already alive and whole.

Strengthen Your Spirit

Jesus, who was a fully spiritual being equal with God, put on the shell of a human body. He was tempted and troubled just as we are. That earthly reality was reflected when He cried out, "My soul is crushed with grief to the point of death…. The spirit is willing, but the body is weak!" (Matt. 26:38, 41 NLT).

Jesus sought the Father's will in the garden of Gethsemane right before He was taken captive to suffer and die on the cross. Scripture reveals that He was so physically and emotionally exhausted, He actually sweated drops of blood (see Luke 22:44). Can you imagine sweating blood from your glands? How quickly would you run to the ER or call your doctor? Though His own disciples seemed to ignore Jesus's witness in the garden, it is absolutely essential for our healing. He didn't run for bandages or reach for numbing substances. He didn't avoid the problem or choose denial. Instead, He strengthened His spirit. He prayed.

You might think, *Well, Jesus is God; it was probably easier for Him.* If that's true, why was He sweating blood? Why did He need to pray? And why did He beg His Father for an easier path when He cried out, "My Father! If it is possible, let this cup of suffering be taken away from me" (Matt. 26:39 NLT)?

Jesus was 100 percent God and 100 percent man. He knows the battle we faced because He faced it too. That's why He said to His sleeping disciples, "The spirit is willing, but the body is weak!" (v. 41 NLT). When His soul was in anguish and His body was about to be broken, He didn't try to fix the broken parts. He focused on His spirit.

It gives me great hope to know that Jesus understands my daily struggle. Hebrews 4:15 explains that "we do not have a high priest who is unable to empathize with our weaknesses, but we have one who has been tempted in every way, just as we are—yet he did not sin." Jesus chose to surrender to His Father's will and obey. You and I have the same choice every day. When we're weak, we can run to the Father, as Jesus did in prayer, and tap into the power of His Holy Spirit, who lives inside us.

The Power of the Holy Spirit

You are never alone. You don't have to fight this daily battle by yourself. God gives you the Holy Spirit to help you. Jesus promised, "I will ask the Father, and he will give you another Advocate, who will never leave you. He is the Holy Spirit, who leads [you] into all truth" (John 14:16–17 NLT). The Holy Spirit is part of the Trinity, which also includes God the Father and God the Son. At the moment of salvation, the Holy Spirit comes to live inside us. The problem is that we often continue operating in the flesh, trying to do things in our own strength rather than tapping into the power of the Holy Spirit. According to Romans 8:6, "The mind governed by the flesh is death, but the mind governed by the Spirit is life and peace."

The challenge is to learn how to walk with the Holy Spirit, who is our firm foundation, instead of letting our wounds batter and bully us.

BATTLE PLANS

I've shared that when Jen first emerged from her coma, her mind and body were completely broken but the Holy Spirit was alive and perfect inside her. She didn't know who she was. She didn't know she was hurt. She couldn't follow a verbal command or answer a question. If we asked, "What is your name?" or "What is your birthday?" or "Who is your best friend?" she didn't know. She didn't even remember that she had a brother! But when we sang praise songs to her, she could sing along and remember every word. One day when Jen was in excruciating pain and couldn't perform a single rudimentary function, like blinking her eyes or rolling onto her side, I started quoting Psalm 23 over her.

When I choked up with emotion and could no longer say the words, Jen miraculously picked up where I left off and finished quoting the chapter. Her first sentences were scriptures she had hidden in her heart as a child. We quickly figured out that if we wanted to communicate with Jen, we had to tap into the Holy Spirit, who was alive in her. It was the only part of her that wasn't injured.

If you've ever watched a loved one emerge from a coma, it's not like in the movies. You don't open your eyes one day and sit up and have a conversation. It can be a horrific process of moaning and thrashing and utter turmoil. It's almost unbearable for a mother to watch. The patient has to relearn everything from swallowing to forming words to walking. Often, as in Jen's case, half of the patient's face is paralyzed, which makes speaking and eating very difficult. At first, words are slurred and unintelligible. That's why I was in awe when Jen started praying. When she prayed, she sounded like the uninjured Jen. Her voice was clear and precise, and she wasn't confused. When Andy and I heard her prayers, it sent chills up our spines. We had never experienced anything like this in our lives. When we tried to talk with her about physical, functional things, she couldn't get her tongue to form the words correctly. But when Jen prayed, it was as if God was healing her on the spot!

Jen would have a two-way conversation with God where she would ask Him a question, wait, listen, and then seem to answer His questions. It was as if she was in God's throne room and we were getting a sneak peek at what was going on in the spiritual realm. The praise songs and scriptures had been memorized when she was well, but when she prayed, she was choosing and organizing her own words. Sometimes she would say things like "Lord, thank You for all the people I have been able to influence." Or "Father, thank You for bringing me to this place to share my testimony."

One day she asked God, "Should I go, or should I stay?" She waited and then replied, "Okay, Lord, but there aren't words to describe You. Please show me what is in this picture, Father. How can I do it?" Then, after a long pause, we heard her say, "It's going to be hard. But yes, Lord, I will do it."

Honestly, it reminded me of Jesus in the garden of Gethsemane. It was as though she was surrendering to her Father's will. Sometimes she would look at us and say things that were so convicting, it was as if God Himself was talking to us. I believe it was her spirit connecting with God's Spirit. There really is no other human explanation.

For Jen to stay in the hospital, our insurance company required her to complete three hours of therapy a day. But she could barely stay conscious for one or two hours. She would wake up moaning and thrashing, and we would pray and sing with her for a few minutes, and then she would go back to sleep for five or six hours. This went on for weeks. Our insurance company threatened to send her home if she didn't start improving faster. The doctors told us that Jen had a flat affect, which meant she had no emotional expression. They also said she couldn't follow any verbal commands. Except, clearly, she was waking up and praying in the middle of the night, praising God with a huge smile on her face and receiving commands from her heavenly Father!

One of her therapists, Miss Penny, figured out that if she could tap into Jen's spirit, Jen would do anything asked of her with great determination. For example, Miss Penny hadn't been able to convince Jen to pick up a pencil and write the three letters J-E-N. Jen would cry and say, "I can't! This hurts! This hurts!" So one day Miss Penny asked her to write "I love Jesus." Jen immediately picked up the pencil and tried her hardest for almost a half hour. The other therapists started to pick up on this success. When she was physically unable to stand, the therapists played her favorite praise music and Jen would stand up and put her arms around their necks and slow dance to the praise music for twenty minutes. It was amazing what she could do. In other words, Jen's broken body and soul could function only by relying on the strength of the Holy Spirit, who was alive and whole in her.

THE FOUR *P*s

Jen was far from ready to come home and function in the real world. The only way to cope and make it through the day was to continue doing what we came to affectionately refer to as the "four *P*s"— *prayer, promises, praise,* and *positivity.* As it was in the hospital, the only progress she was able to make was through the four *P*s.

For example, Jen would be in so much pain that she couldn't get out of bed, and I would say, "Are you doubting God?"

Jen would reply, "Oh no! I would never doubt God."

We would then quote simple verses to encourage Jen to get out of bed, such as "I can do everything through Christ, who gives me strength" (Phil. 4:13 NLT). Over the following months and years, God's Word became life to us. We had Bible verses written out in every corner of our home. We played praise music 24-7. And we had about every book ever published that organized God's promises under headings like *Fear, Anger, Doubt, Healing, Pain,* and *Financial Problems.* Our relatively normal home had transformed into a sanctuary for God's Spirit. We had believed in God and worshipped Him before, but now He filled every corner of our home.

I wish I could say that I was this amazing spiritual giant or super-mom. Honestly, we transformed our home because we had to. We were desperate for God every minute of the day. There were days when I needed God to be able to take my next breath. He was my only chance for survival!

And spiritual communication was my only way to communicate with my daughter. She was so confused. So broken. She couldn't read or do any tasks by herself. The only time she seemed to make sense was when we were singing praise songs, praying, or quoting Scripture. So that's what we did. Over and over and over again.

In those dark days, Jen was the one who pulled me out of the pit. In the midst of all her pain and suffering, she praised God continually. Doctors had warned us that because of the severity of Jen's brain injury, she would be depressed and suicidal. Instead, she was full of inexplicable joy! The first thing she learned to do was to turn on the CD player in the family room. She would blare the praise music to help her cope with her headaches and stomach pain. She danced to praise music. She prayed aloud throughout the day and spoke to Jesus as if He were standing next to her. We continued to quote promises from God's Word out loud with her throughout the day because that enabled her to do things she wasn't able to do in her own strength.

At first we did the four *P*s simply to connect with Jen and make it through the day. Then I started to realize that God was using the four *P*s to heal Jen. In other words, God was offering us more than a coping mechanism. He had given us a healing mechanism that made the spirit greater than the mind and body. It has been ten years, and we still do the four *P*s every day. It's how we do battle for our souls and tap into the living power of the Holy Spirit.

You might be thinking, *Linda, I would love to do the four Ps, but I wouldn't even know where to begin.* Maybe no one ever taught you how to pray, and the thought of praying aloud is frightening. That's why I asked Jen to help me write parts of the next section on prayer to show you the simple steps you can take. She wants you to know that if a girl with a traumatic brain injury can pray, you can too! In the sections that follow, Jen and I also want to give you a peek at what the four *P*s look like in the regular rhythm of our daily lives.

1. PRAYER

Jen wrote in her prayer journal, "I still hurt and struggle every day, but when I pray, God fills me with His strength and courage. God already knows what I need, but He wants me to ask Him. He wants me to draw close to Him and depend on Him for everything. He desires intimacy!"

When Jen showed me what she wrote, I asked, "What do you think about when you're praying?"

She smiled and said, "Well, I often picture God sitting right next to me, and I talk to Him out loud like I would my best friend. He understands my pain. He already knows my thoughts, so I might as well be real and tell Him what I'm thinking. I can even tell God that I hate what I'm going through."

"Yes, Jen," I confirmed. "I love that I can be honest with God too. I can respect Him as holy and still get angry at times. God lets me be who I am. Nothing I say or do will make God stop loving me."

Jen replied thoughtfully, "Praying to God is true freedom. It takes the weight off of me and gives it to the Lord, the One who has the power to heal me and change my circumstances. Even if God doesn't heal me physically, He has healed my soul with His peace that passes all understanding."

I wish you could be a fly on the wall at our house! Every morning Jen rolls out of bed and falls straight to her knees. She surrenders her day to the Lord and says, "God, I know I can't take one step without You."

A few months ago, we were speaking in California. As usual, Jen rolled out of bed in our hotel room and landed on her knees. Wanting to learn from her prayer, I grabbed my iPhone and recorded her: "Good morning, Daddy!" she chimed. "I don't want to miss one plan You have for me today! Please fill me with Your courage and strength. I choose to walk in the power of Your Holy Spirit. I love how You use the weak and incapable for Your glory, so that means You can use me just as I am. Amen."

Now that's the way to start a day!

2. PROMISES

Promises are the truths God gives us in the Bible.

Jen explains, "Reading God's Word is like finding hidden treasures. It's the best part of my day, where God speaks to my heart and answers my questions. God's Word is like a rock! You can stand on it. It is steadfast and never changes. It is absolute truth. It heals!" Psalm 107:20 says that God "sent out his word and healed them."

Following are some promises we use daily in our home to overcome our brokenness. Whenever you're feeling shame, anxiety, or loneliness, try quoting these out loud and watch what God will do.

When you feel *shame* …

> Those who look to him are radiant;
>   their faces are never covered with shame.
>   (Ps. 34:5)

When you feel *anxiety* …

> Cast all your anxiety on him because he cares for you. (1 Pet. 5:7)

When you feel *loneliness* …

> Never will I leave you;
>   never will I forsake you. (Heb. 13:5)

When you feel *unloved* …

> From everlasting to everlasting
> 　　the LORD's love is with those who fear him,
> 　　and his righteousness with their children's
> 　　　　children.
> 　　(Ps. 103:17)

When you feel *unworthy* …

> As far as the east is from the west,
> 　　so far has [God] removed our transgressions
> 　　　　from us. (v. 12)

When you feel *broken* …

> The LORD is close to the brokenhearted
> 　　and saves those who are crushed in
> 　　　　spirit. (34:18)

When you feel *afraid* …

> The LORD is my light and my salvation—
> 　　whom shall I fear?
> The LORD is the stronghold of my life—
> 　　of whom shall I be afraid? (27:1)

When you feel *abandoned* ...

> A father to the fatherless, a defender of widows,
>   is God in his holy dwelling. (68:5)

When you feel *weak* ...

> He gives strength to the weary
>   and increases the power of the weak.
>   (Isa. 40:29)

When you're *tempted* ...

> Submit yourselves, then, to God. Resist the devil,
> and he will flee from you. (James 4:7)

When you need *healing* ...

> LORD my God, I called to you for help,
>   and you healed me. (Ps. 30:2)

When your future is *uncertain* ...

> "For I know the plans I have for you," declares the
> LORD, "plans to prosper you and not to harm you,
> plans to give you hope and a future." (Jer. 29:11)

You can also combine your prayers with God's promises. If you don't know how to pray or what to say, start by praying the promises in His Word. When you pray God's Word, you know you're praying His will. Of course, you can ask God for anything you want, but when you ask Him to do something He has already promised in His Word, you can be sure He will do it.

When I have a problem I can't fix or a circumstance that is out of my control, I search God's Word for verses and promises I can pray and claim aloud over my situation. I know God will answer me because I know I'm praying His will.

Here's an example of a prayer for my friend Susan:

Dear Heavenly Father,

I lift up Susan to You right now. Lord, please fill her with Your peace and Your strength. God, I claim Isaiah 41:10 over Susan right now: "So do not fear, for I am with you; do not be dismayed, for I am your God. I will strengthen you and help you; I will uphold you with my righteous right hand." Lord, please give Susan the courage she needs for the journey.

In Jesus's name. Amen.

I have every confidence that God hears and answers this prayer because it's rooted in His promises. It's a prayer you can pray for your loved ones too.

3. PRAISE

One of the greatest lessons I learned from Jen was to stop begging and start praising God in advance for what He can do. There have been many dark, long nights over the past ten years when I would wake up in a panic and start worrying myself into a downward spiral, thinking of all the things I couldn't fix concerning Jen, our family, or our finances. Many women I talk to admit they can relate. We wake up in the night, and our minds start racing and becoming so anxious that we can't go back to sleep.

One night early in our post-accident journey, I was begging God to fix all of Jen's problems. I couldn't even name them all because there were so many unknowns. Then God reminded me of what Jen was doing in the hospital. She was praising God as if He had already healed her. She knew He was able, and she believed that He would. She would pray, "Lord, thank You for healing me and raising me up." And she couldn't even sit up! She would praise God for hours, worry free, and be full of joy for her future. She would say, "Lord, You are holy, righteous, glorious, triumphant. Lord, I can't even begin to fathom who You are. You are my healer, my best friend, my everything." The list of praise would go on and on, and her face would glow.

So as I was picturing Jen in the hospital praising God, I started singing a praise song in my bed at home. It wasn't a sophisticated praise song; it was one I'd learned as a child: "My God is so big, so strong, and so mighty. There's nothing my God cannot do!" I even did the hand motions and hoped my husband wouldn't wake up and think I was crazy. Then the most amazing thing happened. As I sang that children's praise song, my heart stopped racing, my mind became calm and peaceful, and I fell asleep. That's what happens when we stop begging and start praising!

Have you ever tried singing a praise song to calm your anxious heart? The next time you feel overwhelmed with life, turn on the praise music and try singing at the top of your lungs.

Our family has learned more about the brain than we ever imagined we would. One of the things we learned during Jen's recovery is that music is stored in a different part of our brains than our other memories. What this means is that when your mind is overcome with anxiety in the cognitive-reasoning part of your brain, you can tap into the auditory cortex, where music is stored, to overcome anxiety. That's why Jen was able to sing along with praise songs when she couldn't remember her brother's name. God designed our brains, fearfully and wonderfully, to overcome obstacles and sustain us in the midst of trouble.

Another thing we learned was that we often have dozens of thoughts per minute. That's why you can be praying one second and worrying the next second! I believe this is why praise music is so powerful. I don't know about you, but I'm pretty sure the majority of my thoughts each minute are negative. It's very hard to battle every negative thought. But when I'm singing songs about the truth of who God is, I'm not only engaging a different part of my brain; I'm also capturing four to five minutes' worth of thoughts with the truth about who God is rather than what might happen in the future that I can't really control anyway. Praise takes the focus off our problems and puts it on the power of God.

4. POSITIVITY

I haven't always been positive. I didn't teach this to Jen; she taught it to me. She speaks only positive things out loud. She never says the negative. Her spirit is stronger than her soul. She refuses to think negatively. Whenever I need to hear it, she reminds me, "Mom, sometimes you think too much. If you are struggling, ask Jesus to fill you with His perspective."

A few months ago, we were speaking in Missouri at a women's conference, and I asked Jen on stage, "Why do you speak only what is positive?"

Beaming with her signature grin, she explained, "Say only the positive out loud. Don't say anything negative. What you say is what you believe, and what you believe mentally is how you'll act. If you say the negative, you'll ruin your destiny and give Satan a foothold. God can do anything. You have to believe it. If you say only the positive, there is no limit to what you can do."

In that moment I realized this is exactly what Jen has done for the past ten years.

If I ask her to do something and she has a negative response, she'll immediately come back into the room and apologize. She even apologizes to her brother for the bad or jealous *thoughts* she has toward him! Imagine if we apologized for our bad thoughts. I'd be apologizing every day.

What if we checked our negative thoughts and chose instead to speak only the positive?

Jen will often proclaim with confidence the exact opposite of what I think is true. For example, one Monday she wanted to do something with a friend. I'm ashamed to admit that I was thinking, *Poor Jen. She doesn't really have that many friends, and my friends who would want to spend time with her are probably all busy in the middle of the day.*

One minute later, Jen exclaimed aloud, "I have lots of friends. Now who could I call?"

Jen refuses to think negatively. Sure enough, moments after Jen texted her friend, Melody replied, "I'm dog sitting for two huskies today, and I would love for you to help me take them on a hike up Liberty Mountain."

The next weekend Jen and I were speaking in Hershey, Pennsylvania, at a women's event, and we woke up to no electricity. I was frantic because my hair was wet and I couldn't use my hair dryer or curling iron. When I woke Jen up and told her about the electricity, she giggled and said, "Wow! If there is no electricity, then God is going to do something great today!" She continually turns the negative into a positive.

I asked her how she could continue to be so positive when she has pain in her head and struggles with poor vision and poor memory every day. Her response was overflowing with wisdom.

"I can't keep a negative attitude. It kills me. That is Satan's plan to push us into the pit. When we speak negatively, we ruin our destiny because we start to believe it. I feel guilty when I'm negative, because my spirit knows it's wrong. Satan is the feeder of negative. God is the feeder of positive. God even made the cross positive. He conquered death with it!"

Every day I thank God for what I learn of Him through Jen.

EXPERIENCING WHAT YOU NEVER DREAMED POSSIBLE

Once you begin to implement the four *P*s in your daily routine and continue to speak the words of Jesus on the cross over your wounds, I know you'll experience more healing and more of God's presence. God's Word promises, "By his wounds we are healed" (Isa. 53:5).

Whether your wounds are evident through your wheelchair or as a scar on your forehead or in your heart, God can transform each one into a beauty mark of purpose.

I wouldn't trade the trauma and the long journey toward wholeness because of the beauty of knowing Jesus and experiencing His presence the way I have. He is healing my wounded heart stitch by stitch. Jesus has carried me when I couldn't walk. He has breathed for me when I didn't want to take another breath. Jesus is the reason I get up in the morning. He is my everything! My life on this earth is a dot on the timeline. It is a vapor, a disappearing mist.

One day I'll see Jesus face-to-face, and there will be no more pain or tears. Heaven is more real to me now than the temporal challenges I face. When I see Jesus, it will all be worth it. He is my reward. He is the lover of my soul. Until the day I join Him in heaven, I'm going to tell as many people as I can about His saving grace. That is my passion. That is why I'm still alive. That is my beauty mark!

I know this life can be confusing and painful. Jesus wants to heal your wounded heart. He dreamed of you before you were ever born. He created you, and He loves you. He feels your pain. When you weep, Jesus weeps with you. He collects all your tears in a bottle (see Ps. 56:8). Jesus understands, and He wants to set you free from the wounds of your past. He wants to use you in greater ways because of all you've endured. What Satan intended for evil, God can redeem and use for good. Our beauty marks make us richer and deeper. They make us more than we would have been without them. Wounds changed my family's destiny. God uses us in greater ways because we're broken.

Notice your own heart. Can you recognize your scars as beauty marks? Don't merely *bear* your scars; *wear* them as beauty marks God is using to make a difference in the world He loves.

I'm praying for you. If you're willing, claim this prayer aloud as a declaration of what God is doing today and will do in your future:

Dear Heavenly Father,

I'm coming boldly before Your throne, asking You to fill every broken place and redeem all that the Enemy has tried to steal from me. Lord, I am no longer who I used to be. I am Your treasured daughter. I am priceless, worthy, forgiven, redeemed. I know that You have called me and chosen me for such a time as this to make a difference in my generation. Use me to be a light in a dark world. I am completely abandoned to You. I praise You in advance for healing my wounded heart a little more each day. God, continue to transform my ugly scars into holy marks that reflect Your beauty. I believe You can use my story in ways I never dreamed possible. You can do exceedingly abundantly more than all I could ask or imagine. Help me shine with a hint of Your glory. Daddy, I know that together the two of us can make an impact on the world!

STUDY GUIDE

I'm excited for you to live out the healing journey and incorporate new practices into your everyday life. Grab a journal so you can write notes as God reveals truths to your heart. You can work through this study guide alone in your quiet time with God, but I would encourage you to meet weekly with a friend or small group so you have women you trust covering you in prayer and providing accountability. Some groups meet in person, while others use FaceTime or have private Facebook groups to discuss the study-guide questions with their girlfriends across the country.

Completing the weekly homework, called "Healing Steps," is imperative for making yourself available to God's transforming touch.

Everything you share with one another during your small-group time needs to be kept confidential. And when you share, please don't give the names of people who hurt you or share specific details. For example, you could refer to a friend or close relative but not share the person's name. Or you could say, "I was sexually abused as a child by someone I trusted." You can share your experience and how the wound affected you, but it's wise to save the intimate details for your private time with God.

It's also very important to talk about your wounds in *past tense* instead of present tense when you are able. For example, I was a victim in the past, but I am no longer a victim. God is healing me, and I am hopeful for the future.

Pray and ask God to guide you. He is the almighty healer and the lover of your soul. He already knows everything about you. He will carry you one step at a time.

I'm praying for you. God, who is waiting to receive you, wants to transform the wounded places of your heart into beauty marks of purpose.

IDENTIFY YOUR WOUNDS
AND BEGIN HEALING

Read chapter 1: The Physician No Insurance Company Can Deny

We all have scars and wounds. Some are physical, while others are emotional, hidden inside our hearts. Maybe you came to Jesus and wonder why you still struggle every day. Chapter 1 explains how we are complex creations beautifully made in God's image with a body, soul, and spirit. Whether your wounds happened last week or fifteen years ago, healing is possible! God will help you untangle the mess as you discover the places where you're wounded and apply the healing balm of God's Word.

Here are some definitions that will help you:

Wound: Hurt I experienced

Scar: Evidence I was wounded

Beauty mark: A wound that has been transformed into purpose and evidence that God is redeeming what I've suffered

LET'S TALK

1. Do you have any physical scars on your body? Are you proud of your scars, or do you prefer to cover them up? If you feel comfortable, share your reasons.

2. Why do you think Jesus chose to keep His scars? What does it mean to you and your story that the Creator of the universe has scars?

3. Have you ever felt that the church or God overpromised and underdelivered? Or have you ever felt that God's way has worked for everyone but you? Tell about your experience.

We can look around our church and wonder why everyone has it together but us. We ask, "Why am I still angry and doubting God? Why do I want to give up?" In my journey, knowing that I have a body, soul, and spirit helps me understand why I still struggle. The truth is that many people in church are struggling in the same way we are. Satan wants us to believe we are the only ones.

If you're a new Christ follower, your spirit is alive for the first time. But it may feel as if a battle is raging in your mind and body over your daily choices. We still have our old ways of thinking. Our souls have spent a lifetime gathering beliefs, attitudes, and memories. Perhaps we've even accepted falsehood because it sounded good. Though God sees us as blameless, whole, and redeemed in Christ, our history of brokenness takes time to undo.

Here is a chart to simplify the differences between our bodies, souls, and spirits:

Body	Soul	Spirit
Physiological	Psychological	Spiritual
Sense awareness	Self-awareness	God awareness
Sight, hearing, smell, taste, touch	Mind, will, emotions	Conscience, faith, worship, dwelling place of the Holy Spirit

Body. The body is the physical outer shell God formed out of dust. Our bodies use five senses to relay information from our environment to our brains.

Soul. The soul is the psychological component that includes our minds, wills, and emotions. Our souls allow us to be self-aware and relate to others. The soul is where we struggle with emotional wounds and need Jesus to mend us.

Spirit. The spirit is our inner God awareness that was dead in sin but came to life when the Holy Spirit entered our hearts at the point of salvation. It's what separates humans from the animal kingdom and enables us to commune with God through worship and faith. When the spirit becomes alive in Christ, it enables the soul to be reconciled to God so that soul and spirit will one day be united in a resurrected, glorified body.

READ GOD'S WORD

1. Jesus is our greatest example. Read Matthew 26:37–41 in the New Living Translation. If you don't own a copy, you can find this version at www.biblegateway.com. What did Jesus do when His body and soul were weak?

2. Write out 1 Thessalonians 5:23. How might understanding that you have a body, soul, and spirit help you with your healing journey? How might your spirit be whole and your body or soul be broken? Have you ever experienced this?

PRAYER

Take a moment to write this prayer to God in your journal:

God, will You bring to my attention any wounds from my past or present that You are ready to start healing? Please protect my heart and mind with the power of Your Holy Spirit as You guide me with Your gentle hand. Fill every broken place in my heart with Your truth. I trust You to heal me. In Jesus's name. Amen.

REFLECTION

1. Are you aware of the soul wounds you've endured in the past? Are you currently walking through a painful season of life? In what areas of your life do you recognize the need for God's healing?

2. Do you currently experience any of the ten symptoms of being wounded that were discussed in chapter 1 (also listed below)? Which ones? Take time to evaluate who or what caused them. Write the thoughts God brings to mind in your journal.

You might be wounded if …

- You avoid specific places.
- You avoid certain people.
- You have made a silent inner vow.
- You suffer from emotional triggers.
- You engage in addictive behaviors or have an unhealthy attachment.
- You wound others.
- You experience ongoing, unresolved grief.
- Your thoughts bully you. You feel unworthy, unloved, useless, or disqualified.
- You have a secret you've never told anyone.
- You struggle to verbalize your hurt.

HEALING STEPS

1. If you have any symptoms of being wounded, tell someone you trust—a friend, counselor, family member, or spiritual leader—who could pray for you and walk with you toward healing. If you don't have anyone to tell, start by telling Jesus. Remember, He has scars like you.

2. Healing is possible. Write out this verse on a sticky note, post it where you can see it, and declare it aloud daily for the next six weeks: "'I will restore you to health and heal your wounds,' declares the LORD" (Jer. 30:17).

3. Here are some more healing verses to write out in your journal and claim out loud: Psalm 34:18; 103:2–4; 147:3; 1 Peter 2:24.

ASK GOD WHY AND CHOOSE FORGIVENESS

Read Chapter 2: The Great Cover-Up
Read Chapter 3: Dear Grant …

The first step in the healing process is to open up your wound and ask God why. Jesus gives you permission to ask God why because that's what He did on the cross. He isn't afraid of your hard questions.

Once your wound is open, consider forgiving the person who hurt you. Bitterness spreads. It's a cancer of the soul that tortures you, not the other person. God commands you to forgive for your own physical and emotional health. He wants you to be free.

LET'S TALK

1. Our imperfect parents influence our view of God. What is your view of God? How did your parents affect the image of God you hold in your heart? Do you feel the freedom to approach God and ask why?

2. If you're a parent, or think you might be a parent someday, how do you think the way you're dealing with your past wounds is affecting, or may one day affect, your children? Do you think your current behavior and choices are passing on hope and healing or pain and dysfunction to the next generation?

3. Share at least one thing you learned about forgiveness in chapter 3 that surprised you. What did you discover that forgiveness is *not*?

READ GOD'S WORD

1. Peter, a disciple of Jesus, came to Him asking the question, "How many times do I need to forgive?" Jesus responded with a visual story that's been dubbed the parable of the unmerciful servant. Read Matthew 18:21–35 before answering the following questions.

- Have you ever acted like the unmerciful servant? (I have!) Why do you think Jesus gives you permission to ask God why but doesn't give you permission to withhold forgiveness from those who have wronged you?
- According to this parable and Jesus's example on the cross, how often and when are we supposed to forgive?
- Why is forgiveness so important to your healing? How do you torture yourself over and over by not forgiving?

- Why is it so hard to forgive? Who is the source of forgiveness?

2. When you confess your sins, God forgives you completely. Your debt is marked "paid in full." Write out Proverbs 28:13 and 1 John 1:9 in your journal and thank God for His amazing grace!

3. Once you receive God's forgiveness, He commands you to forgive others. God isn't a bully. He wants what is best for you. When you don't forgive, it hinders your prayers and intimacy with God. Read and reflect on Mark 11:25 and Luke 6:37.

PRAYER

1. Maybe you've been blaming God or condemning yourself for something that happened to you. Would you be willing to forgive yourself today and accept God's grace? Write a prayer to God in your journal, confessing your sins and thanking Him for His forgiveness and full redemption. Psalm 66:18 says, "If I had cherished sin in my heart, the Lord would not have listened." Because unconfessed sin can block your prayers, ask the Holy Spirit to bring to light anything hidden that you need to confess.

2. Isaiah 53:5 declares, "By his wounds we are healed." The words Jesus spoke aloud on the cross have healing power in them. Try praying the things Jesus prayed from the cross out loud right now: *"My God, my God, why have You forsaken me? Father, forgive* _____, *for* _____ *doesn't know what he/she is doing."* Ask God

to show you whose name needs to go in those blanks. Every time that person hurts or offends you, pray these words as quickly as you possibly can. This is how you heal your heart from past wounds and protect it from future wounds. Try praying these words again until you mean them. Rely on the forgiveness your heavenly Father has given you.

REFLECTION

1. Take as long as you need to write down all the names of the people you need to forgive for your own freedom.

2. Because Satan has a counterfeit plan for your life, ask God to show you the lies you've been believing as a result of your wounds. Make a list so you can see the lies and renounce them.

3. The next time you feel unworthy or unforgiven, try saying aloud, "Satan, you are a liar! I have been forgiven for _____. I was washed clean by the blood of Jesus. I choose to believe 1 John 1:7, which declares that 'the blood of Jesus, [God's] Son, purifies us from all sin.'"

HEALING STEPS

Open Your Wound
If you've never opened your wound to God's healing power, try one of the five methods discussed in chapter 2 to ask God why. Jesus has given you permission to approach almighty God and ask freely. Make an appointment with a counselor or spiritual leader today,

talk with a friend, try the empty-chair method, pray, or shout your "Why?" questions to God. He invites you to ask.

Choose Forgiveness

This week write a letter, send an email, or make a face-to-face appointment to forgive your offender. Bury it, send it, say it. However God leads you, finish it! Forgive, expecting nothing from your offender in return and everything from your heavenly Father.

If you're still unable to forgive,

1. Remember that the real enemy is Satan, not your offender.

2. Pray daily for your offender. Ask God to help you pray *blessing* over that person. "Do not repay evil with evil or insult with insult. On the contrary, repay evil with blessing, because to this you were called so that you may inherit a blessing" (1 Pet. 3:9).

3. Put yourself in your offender's shoes. Ask God to give you empathy for that person.

4. Try saying Jesus's prayer again: "Father, forgive _____, for _____ doesn't know what he/she is doing."

If you can't forgive, your Father can.

FIND ETERNAL PURPOSE AND SECURE YOUR SPIRIT

Read Chapter 4: What Does Pain Have to Do with Paradise?
Read Chapter 5: Who Should Hold Your Rainbow Turkey?

Most physical wounds need an antidote or antibiotic to fight off infection and heal completely. The antidote for your emotional wound is to find an eternal purpose in your pain. If you're hurting, your pain can give you a stronger voice to share the gospel. Your heavenly reality is greater than your earthly facts. God will use you in greater ways because of what you have endured.

When you start to relapse into addictive behaviors or your wound is ripped open again, ask your heavenly Father to wrap your wound back up and hold your spirit, the essence of who you are, in His hands. You are always safe in your Father's hands.

LET'S TALK

1. How did you come to know Jesus as your Savior? Did a person or group of people lead you closer to Jesus? Share your story.

2. Has God ever used a difficult circumstance in your life as an opportunity for you to influence someone else's life for eternity? If yes, share how.

3. What has been your most painful experience? Are you able to see a purpose in it, or is it too soon in your healing journey? Share your hopes and your fears.

If you don't have a personal salvation story to tell, today can be your day of salvation! All you have to do is believe in your heart that Jesus died for your sins, ask Him to forgive your sins, and confess with your mouth that you want Him to be the leader of your life.

If you're ready, pray these words from your heart:

Dear God, I confess that on my own I could never earn the right to be with You forever in heaven. I accept the gift of salvation Your Son, Jesus, provided for me on the cross. I repent of my sins, and I invite Jesus to forgive my sins and be the leader of my life. Come live in me and save me. I want to spend eternity with You! In Jesus's name. Amen.

Once you've accepted Jesus as your Lord and Savior, His Holy Spirit comes to live inside you. You don't have to go through life on your own, because the Holy Spirit is now your guide and counselor. He will teach you and remind you of the words of Jesus (see John 14:26; 16:13).

READ GOD'S WORD

1. How are the two martyrs from 2 Chronicles 24:20–25 and Acts 7:55–60 similar? How are they different? What attitudes made the legacy of their painful experiences different? Based on your current attitude and actions concerning your soul wounds, what do you anticipate your lasting legacy will be? Do you think it's possible to influence someone else's eternity because of your experiences? If you could, would it make your pain worth it?

2. Read Psalm 31:4–5. What are some addictions or struggles that tempt you when a wound is reopened? You can entrust your spirit into God's hands by saying out loud what Jesus said on the cross: "Father, into your hands I commit my spirit" (Luke 23:46). How might this prayer be helpful when you relapse or have an old wound torn open again?

3. Jesus tells us how to battle temptation in Mark 14:38: "Watch and pray so that you will not fall into temptation. The spirit is willing, but the flesh is weak." How is this verse relevant to your life this week?

PRAYER

Instead of asking God to heal you today, try praying Jen's prayer: *"Lord, did I meet all of Your expectations today? Did I fulfill all the plans You had for me to do today?"*

REFLECTION

1. Is God birthing a passion in your heart as a result of your own painful experiences? Write about it in your journal.

2. Has God placed a person in your path who might listen to you because of what you've been through? Who is it?

3. Has God revealed a purpose for your life that wouldn't be possible for you to fulfill without the wounds of your past? What is it?

If you don't see any purpose for your pain, try writing this prayer in your journal:

> *Help me hear Your voice, Jesus. You said, "My sheep listen to my voice; I know them, and they follow me" (John 10:27). Speak to me, Jesus, in the way You know I will understand, because You know me. I'll do my best to follow. Give me a purpose for my pain.*

HEALING STEPS

Focusing on my heavenly realities helps me face my earthly facts. For example, one of my earthly facts is that my husband, Andy, and I have chronic nerve pain, but the heavenly reality is that one day we'll have perfect bodies in heaven with no more pain or suffering.

1. Make a list of your current earthly facts and your heavenly realities (see chapter 4).

2. Write out 2 Corinthians 4:17–18 and speak it out loud every day this week: "For our light and momentary troubles are achieving for us an eternal glory that far outweighs them all. So we fix our eyes not on what is seen, but on what is unseen, since what is seen is temporary, but what is unseen is eternal."

3. This week, every time you feel overwhelmed or as though your wound is being ripped open again, pray aloud, "Father, into Your hands I commit my spirit." Did you feel the burden lift after you said these words? Try praying this before you go to sleep.

4. Ask God to save at least one person as a result of your pain. Wait for Him to reveal an opportunity to turn your pain into purpose. Then simply tell your story.

FIND SOMEONE TO SERVE AND SCHEDULE MARGIN

Read Chapter 6: A Cautionary Tale of Two Grandmothers
Read Chapter 7: Ice Chips, Sponge Vinegar, and Living Water

If you're hurting, one of the quickest ways to begin healing is to reach out and help someone else. Serving others helps fill your heart with joy. When Jesus was dying on the cross, He was taking care of His mother's needs, showing her compassion. Jesus also said, "I am thirsty" (John 19:28), which gives us permission to ask for help for our physical needs. It isn't a sign of weakness to ask for help; it's a sign of strength. There are some practical things you can do to add margin to your life, which will give you more time for God and more time for serving others.

LET'S TALK

1. What kinds of activities fill your life bucket and energize you? Shopping? Lunch with friends? Volunteering? A quiet retreat? Reading? What kinds of activities drain your bucket of energy?

Confrontation? Work responsibilities? Overbearing friends or family? Feuds? Cooking? Cleaning? Car pools? Is your bucket currently full or getting close to empty?

2. What are you most passionate about? For example, what breaks your heart and makes you cry? What life-giving activity would you engage in if there was no financial compensation? If you had one year left to live and unlimited resources, what would you do?

3. How many hours a week do you spend volunteering or serving a purpose greater than yourself or your family? What do you experience when serving?

4. When was the last time you unplugged from all technology and social media for an entire day? When was the last time you took a vacation day or spent time listening to God? What was that like for you?

READ GOD'S WORD

1. What were Mary's and Martha's strengths and weaknesses revealed in Luke 10:38–42? Was Martha wrong to focus on her gift of serving? Why is the principle of Sabbath, or margin, important (see chapter 7)? How did Mary exemplify this principle? What are the negative health effects of having little margin in your life?

2. Do you think the Sabbath commandment (Exod. 20:8–11) is possible to keep in today's culture? How could you observe the Sabbath in a way that enables you to spend more time with Jesus? Practically speaking, what would that look like for you?

3. Be honest: Is spending time with Jesus something you view as a chore or something you thirst for? Do you know how to sit at the feet of Jesus? How have you scheduled time for Him in your regular routine?

PRAYER

Offer up this prayer to Jesus and pour out your needs to Him:

> *Jesus, thank You for giving me permission to admit my physical needs by saying, "I am thirsty." Help me find balance in my schedule for serving others and soaking in Your Word. Reveal to me the areas where I need to make adjustments and either serve more or soak more.*

REFLECTION

1. Is there any ministry, person, or opportunity that God is leading you to say yes to?

2. Is there any activity, person, or ministry you need to say no to so you can either have time for Jesus or have time to say yes to another priority? Why do you think God is leading you to say no?

3. Are you currently experiencing any of the following symptoms?

- Chronic fatigue
- Anxiety
- Weight loss or gain (usually ten pounds or more)
- Depression (feeling hopeless, helpless, and worthless)
- Sleeplessness
- Loss of appetite
- Suicidal thoughts

If you have a combination of these symptoms, call your doctor or see a counselor to check on your health, examine the root issues, and set up a recovery plan.

HEALING STEPS

1. Find someone to serve this week. Seek out opportunities to use your gifts, passions, and past experiences to help others. It may be as simple as inviting someone to have a meal in your home, performing an anonymous act of kindness, or visiting a lonely neighbor.

2. Determine to keep the Sabbath by scheduling margin in your life for time with God and things that fill your bucket. Make a Sabbath plan:

- What am I doing *daily*?
- What am I doing *weekly*?
- What am I doing *monthly*?
- What am I doing *yearly*?

3. Take time to celebrate. Think of one thing you could celebrate this week.

Study Guide: Week 5

EXCHANGE YOUR BROKENNESS FOR HEALING AND MAKE YOUR BEAUTY MARK ON THE WORLD!

Read Chapter 8: Accidentally Accessing Bill Gates's Bank Account
Read Chapter 9: Peter, Peter, Peter

It's time to start viewing yourself the way God views you. When Jesus died on the cross and said, "It is finished" (John 19:30), that was the great exchange. Your sins were exchanged once and for all for His righteousness. You are no longer broken; you are righteous, priceless, beautiful, redeemed.

After Jesus's resurrection, He appeared first to a wounded woman (Mary Magdalene) and told her to stop crying. He commanded her to tell the others that He was alive. God wants to restore you at the point of your pain and use you to make a beauty mark on the world. Go share your story and make disciples!

LET'S TALK

1. Describe yourself in three to five words. Where do you find your identity or worth? Is your identity in your job, your outward appearance, or what others think about you?

2. If you were standing face-to-face with God right now, how do you think you would feel?

3. What does it mean to you to realize that the first person Jesus appeared to after His resurrection was a deeply wounded woman?

4. Have you accepted the great exchange? Do you really believe that the way God feels about His own Son is exactly the way He feels about you?

READ GOD'S WORD

1. Read John 18:15–27 and underline in your Bible the words Peter spoke when he denied Jesus. Read John 21:1–17 and underline the words Jesus used to restore Peter. What is the significance of the two charcoal fires in Peter's story? What might this mean for your story?

2. Do you believe that God can fully restore you and use you in the very place where you failed or were wounded? What might that look like?

3. Read Acts 2:38–41 and see what happened when Peter preached at Pentecost. How many people were saved that day?

PRAYER

Pray these words aloud with a Christian friend who can help you see truth:

> *Father God, reveal to me any lies that have festered in my wounded heart or anything I'm believing about my brokenness that isn't from You. Lord, please forgive my failures and help me notice any automatic negative thoughts that abide in me. Help me check every negative thought and replace it with Your truth. I praise You in advance for healing my mind today. In Jesus's name. Amen.*

REFLECTION

God empowers every believer to "demolish arguments and every pretension that sets itself up against the knowledge of God, and … take captive every thought to make it obedient to Christ" (2 Cor. 10:5).

With the help of a friend who knows you well, brainstorm and write down some of your negative thoughts:

1. Look at each thought individually. Is it true? Is there a thought from God that is more true?
2. What typically triggers your negative thoughts?
3. Replace these negative thoughts with truth from God's Word.

Find some promises from the Bible. If you need help with your search, visit www.biblegateway.com and type in words such as *fear, anger, bitterness, hope,* and *temptation* to access Bible verses on these topics. I often print out and highlight the verses that are the most meaningful to me.

HEALING STEPS

Perform a Self-Assessment

Where are you currently on your healing journey? Review the following healing prescriptions Jesus modeled. Which steps do you still need to take to allow God to do more healing in your body, soul, and spirit?

Take a few minutes to perform a self-assessment. Draw an *x* on each line, between zero and ten, to indicate how often you practice each of the healing steps. Zero means "I haven't done this yet," and ten means "I do this well and often."

Open your wound. Ask God why.
"My God, my God, why have you forsaken me?"

0————————————————————————10

Clean out your wound. Forgive your offender.
*"Father, forgive them, for they do not
know what they are doing."*

0————————————————————————10

Apply the antidote. Find eternal purpose
for your pain by sharing the gospel.
"Truly I tell you, today you will be with me in paradise."

0————————————————————————10

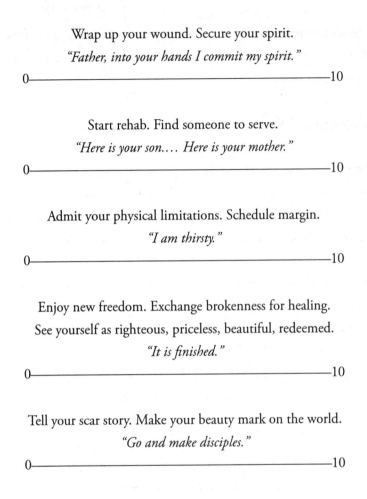

Wrap up your wound. Secure your spirit.

"Father, into your hands I commit my spirit."

0——————————————————————————10

Start rehab. Find someone to serve.

"Here is your son.... Here is your mother."

0——————————————————————————10

Admit your physical limitations. Schedule margin.

"I am thirsty."

0——————————————————————————10

Enjoy new freedom. Exchange brokenness for healing.

See yourself as righteous, priceless, beautiful, redeemed.

"It is finished."

0——————————————————————————10

Tell your scar story. Make your beauty mark on the world.

"Go and make disciples."

0——————————————————————————10

If you can recognize progress as you mark this chart—growth since you began reading this book—it's evidence that God is healing you and can redeem your wounds. Believe it by faith, and praise God that the healing has begun. You can say aloud, "God, thank You for healing me a little more today." If you're not able to notice growth, invite God's Spirit to reveal one area of growth you're being called to embrace. Don't tackle all of them at once; start with one.

Choose a Statement

Write in your journal the statement of Jesus on the cross that has had the greatest impact on your life, and explain why.

Go and Make Disciples

Jesus's final words before He ascended into heaven are known as the Great Commission. In Matthew 28:19–20, Jesus commanded His followers to go and make disciples. Take time this week to write out the story of how God has transformed, or is transforming, your scar into a beauty mark. Pray about how you could share it to help someone else heal.

GOD WANTS TO USE YOU AND HELP YOU WIN THE DAILY BATTLE

Read Chapter 10: Wounded Women Wanted

Read Chapter 11: *P* Is for Power

It's both surprising and beautiful that every woman mentioned in the lineage of Christ was once wounded. Doesn't that give you hope that God can heal you and use you in greater ways because of everything you've suffered? Your body and soul might be broken, but the Holy Spirit, who lives in you, is perfect. Tap into the Spirit's power. The weaker you are, the stronger the Holy Spirit will be in and through you as you win the daily battle practicing the four *P*s (prayer, promises, praise, positivity).

LET'S TALK

1. Which woman in the line of Christ (Tamar, Rahab, Ruth, Bathsheba, or Mary) do you relate the most to (see chapter 10)? Why?

2. When has your brokenness led you closer to Jesus? When has it drawn you farther from Him?

3. Why would a God who has the power to immediately heal you allow you to suffer brokenness and pain? Do you think you would have known Jesus the way you do without brokenness and pain? Has the pain been worth it?

4. Did you learn anything new about the woman who touched the hem of Jesus's garment in Mark 5:25–34? How did she ignite faith in others?

READ GOD'S WORD

1. At the moment of salvation, the Holy Spirit takes up residence in you. Read Romans 8:1–17 and underline all the ways the Holy Spirit can help you win the daily battle for your heart and mind.

Verse 11 says that the same power that raised Jesus from the dead is living inside you. How would you act if you truly believed that?

2. Write out Romans 8:18 and believe it by faith. (This was the verse taped in Jen's locker at school when our car wreck happened.)

PRAYER

Ask God to transform your wounds into beauty marks that He can use to heal others:

God, I don't want to be known as the woman who was
_____ *(name your wound). I want to be known as*

the woman who loves Jesus with all her heart, soul, and mind. Heal me, Lord, from the inside out. Help me to see beautiful instead of broken. Thank You that even though I'm not perfect, Your Spirit is perfect inside me. Lord, please use my story to make a difference in the world!

REFLECTION

1. How can you be led by the Holy Spirit instead of being led by your wounds? How do you think that might be expressed in your life?

2. Satan wants to keep you paralyzed by your past so you won't experience the amazing future God has planned for you. Ask God to reveal other lies the Enemy is using to deceive your soul. Listen to God speaking to your heart and write what He shows you in your journal.

3. Why is it important to combat those lies out loud with the truth of God's Word?

HEALING STEPS

Practice the four *P*s this week:

1. Prayer. *God, Your Word says that nothing is impossible for You. I'm asking You in Jesus's name to heal me and set me free like the woman who touched the hem of Your garment in Mark 5. I believe You can. Please increase my faith to trust You for more healing.*

2. Promises. Find a Scripture verse you can claim to help you battle the particular lies you're tempted to believe. Ask a friend, use www.biblegateway.com, or ask the Holy Spirit to put a promise in your heart today.

3. Praise. *God, I'm going to stop begging You to heal me and start praising You in advance for doing exceedingly abundantly more than I could ever ask or imagine through Jesus Christ!* Now listen to your favorite praise song. Find it online if you need to. Let your spirit lead you as you praise God for the next few minutes.

4. Positivity. Make a list of all the things you're grateful for, even the small things. Then write down some negative thoughts you have about your life. Next to each one, write how God could turn that thought into a positive. For example, next to the negative thought, "I'm afraid that Jen may never be able to live on her own," I might write this positive prayer: "Because of her limitations, Jen has to rely on You more than most girls her age, and I get to see glimpses of You, Father."

How can you implement the four *P*s in your daily routine? Be creative and write an action plan. For example, you can pray aloud in the car, dance to praise music while you're getting dressed in the morning, or memorize promises while you're walking or working out.

Beloved sister, know that God is faithful. He is transforming your wounds into beauty marks so that you might become all He created you to be. Bless you as you continue the journey!

NOTES

1. Rick Warren, "Adding Power to Your Purpose: The Amazing Power of Forgiveness" (sermon, Saddleback Church, Lake Forest, CA, January 7, 2006).

2. Anne Graham Lotz, *Wounded by God's People: Discovering How God's Love Heals Our Hearts* (Grand Rapids, MI: Zondervan, 2013), 52.

3. Mayo Clinic staff, "Forgiveness: Letting Go of Grudges and Bitterness," Mayo Clinic, November 11, 2014, www.mayoclinic.org/healthy-lifestyle/adult -health/in-depth/forgiveness/art-20047692.

4. Matt Carter, "Father, into Your Hands I Commit My Spirit" (sermon, Austin Stone Community Church, Austin, TX, March 2, 2014), http://austinstone .org/resources/sermons/489--father-into-your-hands-i-commit-my-spirit.

5. Mark R. Laaser, George Ohlschlager, and Tim Clinton, "Addictions," in *Caring for People God's Way: Personal and Emotional Issues, Addictions, Grief, and Trauma*, eds. Tim Clinton, Archibald Hart, and George Ohlschlager (Nashville: Thomas Nelson, 2005), 263.

6. Lela B. Long, "Jesus Is the Sweetest Name I Know," public domain.

7. Research cited in Stephen G. Post, "It's Good to Be Good: Science Says It's So," *Health Progress* 90, no. 4 (July–August 2009): 18–25, www.stonybrook.edu /bioethics/goodtobegood.pdf.

8. Albert Barnes, *Barnes' Notes on the New Testament* (Grand Rapids, MI: Kregel, 1962), 354.

9. Vicki Courtney, *Rest Assured: A Recovery Plan for Weary Souls* (Nashville: Thomas Nelson, 2015), 103.

10. If you'd like to see this video of Jen, visit Hope Out Loud, http://hopeoutloud .com/2016/06/30/newsletter-june-2016/.

11. Tom Kelley and David Kelley talk about this issue in their book *Creative Confidence: Unleashing the Creative Potential within Us All* (New York: Crown Business, 2013), 6.

12. Ed Hindson and Ed Dobson, eds., *The Knowing Jesus Study Bible: A One-Year Study of Jesus in Every Book of the Bible; New International Version* (Grand Rapids, MI: Zondervan, 1999), 154.

13. Richard Lee and Ed Hindson, *No Greater Savior* (Eugene, OR: Harvest House, 1995), 269.

14. Caroline Leaf, *Switch On Your Brain: The Key to Peak Happiness, Thinking, and Health* (Grand Rapids, MI: Baker Books, 2013), 37.

15. Daniel G. Amen, "3 Quick Steps to Stop Negative Thinking Now!," The Daniel Plan, November 8, 2016, www.danielplan.com/blogs/dp/3-quick-steps-to-stop-negative-thinking-now-2.

16. Daniel G. Amen, *Change Your Brain, Change Your Life: The Breakthrough Program for Conquering Anxiety, Depression, Obsessiveness, Lack of Focus, Anger, and Memory Problems*, rev. ed. (New York: Harmony Books, 2015), 156.

17. "Dr. Jerome Lubbe," Thrive Neuro Health, www.thriveneuro.com.